W9-AFZ-593

THE MYTHOLOGY OF HORSES

THE
MYTHOLOGY
OF HORSES

Horse Legend and Lore Throughout the Ages

GERALD AND LORETTA HAUSMAN

THREE RIVERS PRESS
NEW YORK

Copyright © 2003 by Gerald and Loretta Hausman

All rights reserved. No part of this book may be reproduced or transmitted in any
form or by any means, electronic or mechanical, including photocopying, record-
ing, or by any information storage and retrieval system, without permission in
writing from the publisher.

Published by Three Rivers Press, New York, New York.
Member of the Crown Publishing Group, a division of Random House, Inc.
www.randomhouse.com

THREE RIVERS PRESS and the Tugboat design are registered trademarks
of Random House, Inc.

Printed in the United States of America

Design by Cynthia Dunne

Art by Mariah Fox

Library of Congress Cataloging-in-Publication Data
Hausman, Gerald
The mythology of horses : horse legend and lore throughout the ages /
Gerald & Loretta Hausman.—1st ed.
p. cm.
1. Horse breeds. 2. Horses—Folklore. 3. Horses—Mythology. 4. Horses in
literature. I. Hausman, Loretta. II. Title.

SF291.H35 2002
398.24'5296655—dc21   2001052520

ISBN 0-609-80846-X

10 9 8 7 6 5 4 3 2 1

First Edition

Acknowledgments

Thanks to Tesuque, New Mexico, horse handler, wrangler, and team driver Sid Hausman, whose forty years of experience in the horse trade attest to an uncommon knowledge of western horse lore. As a former film wrangler and team driver for Warner Brothers, he acquired a lot of practical experience with all kinds of equines. His interviews and stories are in the chapters on the mule, the Appaloosa, the mustang, the Tennessee walking horse, the Morgan, and the Belgian.

Karen D. Rickenbach helped us with research and with the chapter on the Connemara pony, and we wish to extend to her our deepest appreciation. Dianne Tidwell gave us insight and research assistance on the Morgan and the paso fino. Hannah Hausman and Grace Pedalino contributed material on various breeds. As always, special thanks to the staff of the Pine Island Public Library. The drawings in the book are by illustrator Mariah Fox; we are grateful to her for her contributions to this and our other mythology books.

Contents

Introduction

THE HORSE IN FLIGHT

The horse, like the dog and the cat, has been an important—if some-times reluctant—counselor of compassion, kindness, cleverness, courage, and the art of four-footed deliverance since the earliest times with human beings.

But whereas the dog and the cat have been agreeable bedfellows, so to speak, and secret sharers of our soul, the horse—in size alone—has kept her distance from us. Yet apart from humankind, the horse was no less than what she has always been—an independent wonder, an order of being altogether different in shape and psyche from ourselves.

Or was she?

In the horse we can see the sacred history of ourselves, our passage through time as warrior, priest, healer, wrecker of worlds, and builder of dreams. We can see it all in the horse's eye; in the prism of her pupil is our beginning and, perhaps, our end.

Truly, she contains the cosmos of collective memory.

In her magnitude, there is a vast repository of wisdom.

In the magic whorls of her brain is encoded the course of humankind's folly, fantasy, determination, failure, and ingenuity.

Canine mythology explains that God, seeing Man so feeble, gave him Dog so that he wouldn't be so miserable.

Feline mythology suggests that we couldn't see God—but we could see, and worship, Cat.

Equine mythology says that Man was once Horse. Naturally, that is not the end of the story.

The five-thousand-year cycle of equine myths shows that when a human becomes one with a horse, what transpires is just as Shakespeare remarked,

> *more than one,*
> *And yet not many.*

What *is* it, then?

For lack of a better word, magic.

The cat and the dog got us safely down the path, but the horse took us through the hedge and out into the gloried and storied magic wood. In going off on her back, we discovered, however, that the thing we sought was already with us: It was Horse herself.

The mythology of the horse is, in fact, this ancient wild ride on the back of that old, familiar mare of the night, Nightmare. A gallop through the centuries of mysticism, alchemy, flight, and fable teaches us that the mount is seldom ennobled by the rider, but it's almost always the other way around.

As horsemen—whether Don Quixote, Don Juan, or Jeanne d'Arc—the human in us rises to a greater sense of self and is indeed bettered and brightened by virtue of the horse's dignity and equanimity. In this instance, we have only to remember Comanche, the sole survivor of the Seventh Cavalry, that singular, historic horse that survived the Battle of the Little Bighorn, standing faithfully beside his fallen man days after the last bullet had been fired.

The oral literature of the equine takes us astride into our own dim past and shows us our darker self. Yet it's also true that on horseback we can see humanity emerge—not always as a self-defeated warrior with a *sword*, but as an invincible warrior with a *dream*.

On horseback—so say our myths—we shall live forever.

Equine tales remind us to "let go of the reins, and fly!"

For it is then, in that instant of letting go, that we are finally freed of our burden to enter our destiny, that which is indivisible from that cosmic horse. Long ago, mythology says, we were once joined in bone and sinew, in spirit and flesh to all that is equine.

In the long ago—just a moment ago—we were born in the body of a horse. Big-hooved and bighearted, we trod upon the Milky Way, kicking hot sparks at the cold moon.

Moments ago, we were four-footed gods.

I

AFRICA

1

The Horse of Muhammad

ARABIAN

The Arabian horse came out of the great deserts of the East, but equine experts do not know precisely where any more than etymologists know the origin of the word *Arab*, which remains a mystery to this day. Yet over the centuries the stunning desert horse and the nomadic Bedu have become nearly synonymous.

Indeed, the Arab horse was hot-blooded; so was her master. The horse was the wind, and her master put a bridle to it.

As it says in the Koran, the Bedu horseman was a refined instrument of war, a wielder of death to all infidels; "By the snorting war steeds, which strike fire with their hoofs as they gallop to the raid at dawn and with a trail of dust split apart a massed army; man is ungrateful to his Lord! To this he himself shall bear witness" ("The Chargers" [100:1–7]).

The great horse probably existed on the Arabian Peninsula around 2500 B.C. The mystery of the Arabian's origin is certified by the extreme aridity of the desert climate; she couldn't have lived in the interior of the Arabian Peninsula without the aid of people.

Where did she come from?

"In the beginning there was a wild horse, and that horse was man. . . ." So goes the oldest of Babylonian myths. So the equine didn't come before man but at the same time. This is to say that the Arab people have not been known longer than the Arabian horse has been known. Actually, the name *Arab*, a Semitic word, refers not to a race or nationality but to an inhabitant of the desert, one who is either from the valley of the Nile or the steppes of southern Turkey.

In any case, the Arabian horse was bred some 3,500 years ago and raised as "a drinker of the wind, a dancer of fire," the Arab poets say. According to the Emir Abd-el-Kader, a nineteenth-century Arab king, the lineage of breeders is as celebrated as the horse. And it goes from Adam to Ishmael, from Ishmael to Solomon, and from Solomon to the prophet Muhammad.

Ishmael, the cast-out son of Abraham and maybe the first Bedu tribesman, bred and refined the Arabian stock. An even earlier breeder, though, was Baz, the great-great-grandson of Noah. The archetypal mare Baz was named after him and bred to the stallion Hoshaba.

The Bedu horse breeders were an odd lot of belligerent yet congenial people. They would accept a desert guest as if he were a family member. The unwritten code of honor called for a traveler to be honored and fed in camp, and this included his entourage and his animals, which could number in the hundreds.

All a visitor had to do was touch a Bedu tent pole, and he became a welcome guest. His horse's bridle was then hung from the highest part of the tent to show the great respect the stranger was going to be given.

Thus did the tribes find themselves in the company of other horsemen like themselves. These were men with whom they shared secrets and passions and for whom they suspended ancient tribal disputes. In this way, the Arabian horse became a healer of nations. Not only did she transport the guest to the host, but she would often become the mother of blooded foals that united everyone. So peace was achieved when a desert wanderer and his horse came into a strange camp and found a haven from the sun.

In time, the pact was sealed by stallion, mare, and foal.

The Bedu raced their best horses, and the winners of these races got the finest stock from the loser's herd; this diversity made champion racers, horses of myth, well groomed and proud. An unknown Arab poet of long ago wrote, "The nostrils of a racer are like petals of a rose. . . . The neck is an elongated wave from which floats brilliant ripples of silken mane. . . . The ears, inward pointing, are lilies in trembling water, and the whole body of the mythical, yet fleshly, horse sways with the supple strength of wind, sun, and sand."

King Solomon disregarded the Israelite law that forbade the keeping of horses. He encouraged horse breeding by building stables for forty thousand horses of Arabian blood. Some of these were taken by King Solomon's son Menyelek, who bore the sacred Ark of the Covenant from Judah to his home in Ethiopia.

Menyelek's caravan traveled, they say, as if upon the wind. The sacred text the Kebra Nagast tells us it was watched over by angels:

> Upon his command the king himself rose up and followed the road taken by the men of Ethiopia; and the mounted horsemen who went with him rose hard ahead and, at last, came to the country of Egypt. The soldiers of King Solomon questioned the people there, and the Egyptians said to them, "Some days ago the travelers you seek came by here in wagons which moved swifter than the eagles of the heavens."

Mythology has woven a tangled web about the feet of Solomon— a snare from which he couldn't extract himself. He loved horses and wanted a great stallion, but he had to break Moses' decree—"The king shall not multiply horses to himself"—to get what he wanted. Yet when he broke the command of Moses, he forgot the hour of evening prayer—and *this*, according to Muhammad, brought on Solomon's downfall.

However, we also know he had other problems—his wife, for instance. He married the Pharaoh's daughter. She worshiped idols— golden insects, fish, and *horses*. In the Koran, Solomon laments, "Truly, I have loved the love of earthly good above the remembrance of my Lord, until the sun hath been hidden by the veil of darkness. . . ."

Sunlight and horses. The two are expressive of divine grace in Arabic literature and, indeed, the horse of the sun is one of the oldest metaphors of mythology.

Equine sacrifices were done to glorify the sun. Ancient horses figure largely in solar rites. The Greek writer Xenophon said that the Persians and Armenians made horse sacrifices, as did, of course, Solomon.

Horses were put to death and dismembered, and at the same time, live equines were chosen for their beauty and harnessed to white chariots. They were crowned and consecrated. Mares became sun horses by learning solar dance patterns, including one that is, strangely enough, practiced by some Native American tribes to this day.

Muhammad's influence on horse breeding doesn't have the complexity of Solomon's, but it proves the horse's high status in Arab society. Muhammad was single-handedly responsible for reshaping the Arab nation; he changed his followers from sheep and camel herdsmen to horse warriors who, if they should be slain in battle, would be given eternal bliss in paradise.

Moreover, Allah would indulge sins. All a sinner had to do was give a grain of barley to a horse. Muhammad also proclaimed that the horse's back was the human seat of honor. Yet how this back was chosen is an allegory all by itself. According to horse expert Stan Steiner *(Dark and Dashing Horsemen)*:

> Even after Muhammad had built a stable full of horses, it says in the Koran that he did not entirely trust them. He decided to test their loyalty by depriving one hundred horses of any water for three days, and when they had been maddened with thirst, he let the horses go to find water. As they stampeded he ordered that the horn of battle be blown. Most of the crazed horses ignored it; there were only five, all mares, who answered the Prophet's call and trotted obediently to his side. These five became the Five Mares of the Prophet, his most loyal mounts, and their foals alone were honored by the name *asil*, Arabian horses of "pure blood."

Arabian horses were therefore given the best and most royal respect. They slept in tents with their masters and mistresses, and they ate from their bowls. Owning a horse and caring for it was a sacrament, an Islamic virtue praised in Muhammad's book of rules, the *Hadith*. Muhammad was the one therefore who developed the original test of mare fidelity. A breeder of Arabians in the nineteenth century got an unridden filly and rode her across rocks and hot sand at full speed for sixty miles. Afterward—with no rest—she was forced to swim for a period of time, and if after completing this exhausting ordeal she would still eat as if nothing had happened, then her breed was determined to be pure.

Muhammad's personal horse was named Al Borak, which means "lightning" in Arabic. This mythical white-winged mare was said to have a human head, thus proving the ancient metaphysical belief that horses and men were once joined.

After Muhammad's death in A.D. 632, his followers said that he was borne to the Seventh Heaven on the back of Al Borak. Following the passing of Muhammad—in the years that succeeded the actual event of his death—mounted Muslim armies conquered half the known world, spreading east and west until they were finally defeated, one hundred years later, by the Frankish knight Charles Martel.

When Islamic rule ended, the Arabian horse began to travel out of Arabia into the world at large. Martel started his own breeding program, and this, in fact, was facilitated by the invention of the firearm. The loss of heavy armor and the horse that carried it made way for the new knight, who rode an Arabian-blooded horse and carried a long gun.

The Crusades brought bloodstock to England and France, and at its culmination, three crucial Arabian stallions—the Darley Arabian, the Byerly Turk, and the Godolphin Arabian—founded the Thoroughbred breed between 1690 and 1728. In the time of Louis XIV, the Arabian was so sought after that a French consul in Arabia had to beg in order to buy one for his king. The Arab owner of the horse sought by the consul had scarcely a rag with which to cover himself. His children were starving and his house was a shambles, yet he held on to his horse. He was offered gold for the animal. Weeping, he spoke these words: "To whom is it I shall yield thee up? To Europeans who will tie thee close—who will beat thee—who will render thee miserable? Return with me, my beauty, my jewel, and rejoice the hearts of my children."

The European horse soldier was enchanted by Arabian myths, and he subscribed easily to the myth of the sun horse. Christopher Marlowe, echoing the poets of Persia, wrote,

The horses that guide the golden eye of heaven
And blow the morning from their nostrils.

In midsummer, medieval bonfires blazed with the wooden head of a horse carved in effigy. In Russia, a bridle cut from the bark of a linden tree was burned as a sacrament. These pagan bonfires were usually built in front of the town church to please the clergy, and they did, for a time.

Yet all of this pageantry came from the Arabian horse. She gave nobility to battlefield and ballad, bas-relief and personal prayer. No horse cast more holy sparks into the world of Christendom. No horse had more sun in her or more history or more religion than the wild horse of Ishmael, which came out of the desert to serve mankind.

The Characteristics of the Arabian

The Arabian is finely crafted, with a short head that in profile shows a concave or dished face. The forehead is convex, forming a *jibbah*, or shield shape. The horse's small muzzle is said to ideally fit into a person's hand. The eyes, deep and large, are thought to be soulful in the mare and wisely alert in the stallion.

Upper equine beauty is defined by a high-set arched neck. A naturally lofty tail determines perfection in the hindquarters. The Arabian's chest is muscular and broad, and the legs, although delicate-looking, are strong, ending in small, articulate hooves. Height is between fourteen and fifteen hands. The fine, silky coat is chestnut, bay, and black, often with white markings on face and legs.

Keen intelligence is perhaps the best-known quality of this remarkable equine, but this is also a horse of great swiftness and endurance. On the trail and in the ring, the Arabian excels as a mince-footed dancer with no equal. The sum total of greatness in the Arabian is not just her incredible beauty—it is her ability to bond with humans.

This cardinal feature comes from thousands of years of genetic coding. These horses, like the Great Danes of canine lore, bedded down with their owners and supped with them. Indeed, a visitor to an Arab tent once remarked that the horse lay dozing in the center of the family enclosure with sleeping children sprawling upon its shoulders, flanks, and neck.

2

The Horse of Babylon

DOMESTIC ASS

T he horse of Babylon, the ass, came from Africa, and the Assyrians who made so much of her were barefoot, spur-wearing horsemen who charged into battle bareback, as skillful as any warriors that ever were.

In Africa and the desert regions of the Middle East, the horse was so sacred that some tribes did not ride at all. Stan Steiner *(Dark and Dashing Horsemen)* says that only the gods had the privilege of riding. Men and horses were seen as brothers, not just men and mounts.

So the presence of the dun-coated donkey, the lowly but not unloved ass, is greatly misunderstood in our time. Steiner underscores this: "Asses and donkeys were not then thought of as animals to be ridiculed as we might think of them today. They possessed the nobility that humans always attribute to creatures upon whom they depend for survival."

The *Book of Abiquar*, written in the fifth century, records that "a man said to a wild ass one day, 'Let me ride you and I will feed you,' whereupon the ass replied, 'Keep your fodder and may you never ride me.'"

The independence of the ass notwithstanding, the riding got off to such a good start that thousands of donkeys were used to haul the caravans that we read about in the Old Testament. There might be several thousand asses for a single desert caravan. Masters of such caravans depended on what we might call Hebrew cowboys—ropers, breakers, and rounders who really did know the ropes, so to speak.

Indeed, the very word *Hebrew* comes from *apiru*, or *abiru*, which means "donkey driver" or "caravaneer."

Enkidu, the rough and uncivilized pal of Gilgamesh, was said to be the son of a gazelle mare. His father was a wild ass of the hills. Overall, both biblical and secular literature of Asia Minor shows that for many centuries the ass was more vital than the horse. By the time of Gilgamesh, 2,000 B.C., the equine had, however, evolved into the indispensable mount of the warrior, and—bingo—civilians were ass owners, and the military were horsemen.

Long before this, though, the domestic ass of North Africa had a history longer than its ears. In Egypt and Mesopotamia, asses were standard saddle animals and beasts of burden and, incidentally, women rode them more than men. You have to search the Bible painstakingly for any mention of horses. In the Ten Commandments, for instance, no horse talk. But remember the line—how could you forget it?—about coveting your neighbor's ass?

In ancient Syria there were four kinds of ass: the light and graceful kind reserved for women; the Arabian breed with saddle for men; the heavy-muscled variety for field- and farmwork; and the large, long-eared Damascus ass for general use.

Of the four, perhaps the most notable is the Arabian. A man who maintained a fine stable of these was indeed a wealthy man. Bridles were ornate and decorated with bells, silken cords, fringe, shells, and small rosettes—the pretty accoutrements we associate with an Arabian horse. Saddles were just as elaborate, with stirrups of costly metal and ornaments of rich design.

The respect given the ass was not only as a beast of burden, but also as a show animal. In John Leo's *Descriptio Africae*, a sixteenth-century memoir, the ass is described as a wise fool, a creature of foolery and finery and fun:

> The dancing of the ass is diverting enough, for after he has frisked and capered about, his master tells him that the Soldan [sultan] means to build a great palace and intends to employ all the asses in carrying mortar, stones, and other materials; upon which the ass falls down with his heels upwards, closing his eyes and extending his chest, as if he were dead.

After this, the master begs money from his audience to compensate him for the death of his ass. As soon as he has a purse full of coins, he explains that his animal is really alive and well. The clever fellow remains still, however, continuing to trick the audience.

Finally, the master tells the people that by edict of the sultan, all ladies shall ride upon a train of beautiful asses. At this the performing beast jumps to its feet and wiggles its ears to be ridden. No animal, short of a monkey or a bichon frise, has more effectively fleeced a bunch of bystanders than the Arabian ass of ancient times.

William Shakespeare was mindful of this, too, when he scripted the character of Bottom in *A Midsummer Night's Dream*. Bottom is no mere ass, but like the character of old, plays many parts, and at the outset of the play he begs to do them all. He offers to roar like the lion and beard himself as well. Of the beard, he promises bright blooms of a dozen shades—straw, tawny, purple-in-grain, French-crown, etc. Basically, what he says is that he will be whatever is asked of him. He will play all of his parts so well that no other actors shall be necessary. He will even throw the voice of the nightingale, if need be.

This, without a doubt, is the Damascus ass, the clown of the ancient East, who says, "I grant you, friends, if that you should fright the ladies out of their wits, they would have no more discretion but to hang us: but I will aggravate my voice so that I will roar you as gently as any sucking dove; I will roar you an 'twere any nightingale."

Since the ass has been made the literal butt of so many jokes, we should explain what the expression "half-ass" really means. First, if the poor animal had not been indispensable, the gibes would not have been so funny. Second, if the stable had not been the inn of choice where one lay down with the ass, we might not have had any joke at all. Science, believe it or not, gets into the bargain, too.

Zoologically, the Asian ass is a hybrid; it has the nature of both horse and ass and some of its own distinctive features as well. Its being neither horse nor ass, though, led to its being called half-ass, or what is the equivalent of the saying "neither fish, nor fowl, nor good red herring."

According to *The Encyclopedia of the Horse*, one of the hominid breeds, the Kulan of Mongolia, is able to run at speeds of forty miles per hour, faster than their natural predators, the desert wolves, and also faster than a Thoroughbred racehorse. One such stallion averaged a speed of thirty miles an hour for more than sixteen miles. What, we ask, is half-assed about that?

The donkey and the ass have been used and abused over the centuries, and yet in our literature these two trumps are steadfast and

THE HORSE OF BABYLON ■ 15

enduring not only as beasts of burden but as intelligent creatures with superlative insight. Take, for instance, the well-known tale "The Bremen Town Musicians" by the Brothers Grimm. In this story it is the donkey who is fed up with the way he is treated. And his decision to break away and become his own person is a bitter comment on humankind's unkind treatment of him and his kin.

> A donkey had for years faithfully carried his master's sacks of wheat to the mill for grinding. But the donkey was losing strength and was able to work less and less. His owner had about decided the animal was no longer worth his keep, when the donkey, realizing that no kind wind was blowing in his direction, ran away. He took the road to Bremen. Once there, he thought, he would become a town musician.

Throughout the fable the donkey is staunchly the idea man, the impetus, the inciting force behind the other animals' rebellion. He instructs the others—the cock, the dog, and the cat—giving them reason to believe they can succeed, as animals, by themselves. True, they are domesticated versions of what they once were. But, so the donkey tells them, they are free souls with talents of their own. Characteristically, the mindful donkey never lets them down, nor does he allow his vision of becoming a musician fail him or his friends. He is, in fact, the hub of their universal order, their march to Bremen Town.

In exchange for the donkey's practical wisdom, his furred and feathered friends give him their utmost loyalty. Always, this is rewarded with the donkey's insight. As the tallest member of their clan, he sees more than they do, and this, we suspect, is more than sight. It is, as the Zen masters say, seeing into things.

> The donkey, as the tallest, went to the window and peered inside.
> "What do you see, Grayhorse?" asked the cock.
> "What I see," replied the donkey, "is a table loaded with lovely food and drink. And the thieves are sitting around it, enjoying themselves."

"That would be something for us," said the cock.

"Yes, indeed. If only we were inside," said the donkey.

The donkey's calm certainty and common sense are, to coin a phrase, almost human. In fact, they are the virtues of independent thinking, the exact opposite of what the donkey is supposed to be as a beast of burden. The cock, most appropriately, calls him Grayhorse, which in a sense denies his identity as a lower-than-horse sack-carrier. The name confers dignity, and the donkey in the moral tale certainly deserves his fair share. Moreover, we notice in the story that whenever the scene is viewed from a linear fashion, Grayhorse sees it differently, fully fleshed, as it were, and multidimensional.

Naturally, the donkey, in psychic terms, represents our untroubled self, our patient, virtuous, communal person. He is the pater, the universal spiritual guide, and yet for millennia he has had to haul us around, and mostly without praise for his diligence and patience.

Christ's triumphal entrance into Jerusalem as King of the Jews was on the back of a donkey, symbolizing his choice of the common lot of man and beast. However, riding on a donkey means more than one thing, and our fables tell us that to sit on the back of one so smart is to be sight-full, as well as in-sight-full, and, oh, so patient and empathic at the same time. So, hail to the little gray horse whose inner wisdom lightens and brightens the darkest path.

The Characteristics of the Domestic Ass

Domestic asses differ from horses most of all in their conformation. The ears are extremely long in proportion to the size of the head, the necks are straighter, and most of them lack a true withers. Because of the lack of withers, their backs are straighter than those of horses. The mane and tail are coarse, and the mane is upright, while the tail is covered with stiff hair and ends in a tasseled switch more like a cow. They do not have a true forelock. Their coats are dun-gray, brown, white, chestnut, bay, black, roan (both red and gray), white, and sometimes a uniquely spotted pattern similar to the Appaloosa.

They have dorsal stripes and dark ear points as well as white muzzles and eye rings; donkeys may have zebra stripes on their legs. The size of the donkey is greatly variable. The miniature Mediterranean is only thirty-six inches, but the mammoth jackstock is fourteen hands and up. The rare French Poitou, with its huge shaggy head and curled black coat, is considered a giant at fifteen hands. The standard size is forty-eight to fifty-four inches, and a large standard would stand fifty-four to fifty-six inches. Donkeys can gait just like horses, although galloping is usually not their favorite form of locomotion. They also make excellent "guard asses" because they have a natural aversion to predators, especially feral and domestic dogs, coyotes, foxes, and wolves.

All asses and donkeys have a distinctive voice, a raspy bray. Jacks especially enjoy sounding off.

3

The Hittite Horse

MULE

T he mule is that anomaly, a cross between a mare and a male donkey that cannot sire his own offspring. The sadness of this may have led us to believe that the mule is sort of a "dead end" of the equine kingdom. Nothing, however, could be further from the truth. Biologically, the mule is a halted thing, but spiritually, he comes from a long, if interrupted, line of ingenious, curious, and almost unaccountably smart fellows. History has marked him otherwise, giving him an archetypal bad rep that goes back to one of our oldest of documents, the African bible known as the Kebra Nagast. The eighth-century Ethiopian text speaks of the mule in its earliest chapter:

> And the wickedness of the children of Cain multiplied, until at length in the greatness of their filthiness they introduced the seed of the ass into the mare, and the mule came into being, which God had not commanded even like those who give their children who are believers unto those who deny God, and their offspring become the seed of the filthy Gomorraites, one half of them being good and one half of them being of evil seed.

The condemnation is not really against the mule but rather the *idea* of the mule. The real culprit is man: human interference with divine intention. Interestingly, the Kebra Nagast refers to the concept of genetic implanting, the creation of a new form of life that cannot reproduce itself. So the mule's bad rep—and rap—starts here, where it got known as a dumb, stubborn, hardy, foolish friend of man.

And nothing could be further from the truth.

To this day, it is imagined that the Kebra Nagast was revised and editorialized by Arabian scribes, who may very well have been putting down the mule to raise up the horse, which had been sanctified by Muhammad. Actually, the Amhara people of Ethiopia rode mules, as did the kings of Israel. The Hittites, the most powerful horse people of ancient times, valued mules at three times the price of a horse.

Huge draft mules in Europe were bred carefully over the centuries by crossing an ordinary donkey with a Poitevin, a massive mare from the Poitou region of France. The result was the *baudet de Poitou*, an enormous mule whose value was immediately established in Portugal, Turkey, Greece, Italy, Spain, and the south of France. Today there is a limited revival (with no shortage of buyers for stock), but shortly before World War II, the Poitou region produced thirty thousand mules per year. The price for this horsy-looking, mighty beast was higher than for any other mule on the continent.

In the United States, the Poitou was nicknamed "the Mule That Made America Possible." In reality, that mule, the so-called American Standard, was the famous forty-acres-and-a-mule variety—in short, any draft mule at all. But, mainly, it was the Poitou.

On all fronts, however, American culture was dependent on this singular labor-intensive animal. Land was only as valuable as the mule that carved it with a plow. In effect, good soil meant good mule. Some historians go so far as to say that the southern delta might never have been reclaimed from the sea without the hard-hoofed, strong-hearted mule. Man and animal, each in his own way, was badgered and beleaguered "by a continuous sawing of heartless dust-and-dew-laden cotton reins," one southern writer put it. In *Pills, Petticoats and Plows*, Thomas D. Clark wrote:

> Over a hill trailed a man behind a mule drawing a plow. Unexpectedly the plow hit a root, the mule stopped, and the man began to grumble as he fixed the hames; "Bill, you are just a mule, son of a jackass, and I am a man made in the image of God. Yet here we work hitched up together year after year. I often wonder if you work for me or if I work for you. Verily, I think it is a partnership between a mule and a fool, for surely I work as hard as you, if not harder. Plowing or cultivating we cover the same distance, but you do it on four legs and I on two, therefore I do twice as much as you.
>
> Soon we will be preparing for a corn crop. When the corn is harvested I give one third to the landlord for being so kind as to

let me use a small speck of God's earth. One third goes to you, the rest is mine. You consume all your portion, while I divide mine among seven children, six hens, two ducks, and a store-keeper. If we both need shoes, you get 'em. You are getting the best of me and I ask you, is it fair for a mule, the son of a jack-ass, to swindle a man, the lord of creation, out of his substance?

After World War II, mule production fell off and the breed declined almost to the point of extinction. In 1977, for instance, there were only 44 Poitou mules left in France. However, dedicated breeders brought it back, and though there are now around 180 purebred Poitous, that number needs to be increased to sustain the breed.

Owing to his hardiness on the trail, the mule went out West, car-rying prospector, field hand, and farmer alike. Trains of mules hauled wagons of goods, and before the advent of the steam-driven train, the mule was the standard tool for hauling, lifting, lugging, and log-ging. In short, he was an all-purpose, "handy as a pocket" provider of utilitarian means.

He would go anywhere and do anything: into pitch-dark mine shafts; into canyons and crevices; into water that was shallow or deep, salt or fresh. Basically, the mule took humans where they feared to tread on foot alone.

All during the nineteenth century, this gracious animal was a working angel. He was also a watchdog, as good as a goose and as mean as a dog. In camp and cabin, the mule was brave, and his hand-some face contained a greater nobility to the workingman and -woman than the finely engraved head of the blooded Thoroughbred.

Nor was the celebrated mule ignored in our noblest literature. From Mark Twain to Zane Grey, the mule sat on a high throne of praise. However, it was in *Francis, the Talking Mule* that this animal became a 1950s icon. The popular children's book series was a suc-cession of popular films, too, and, incidentally, the screen voice of Francis was Chill Wills, the cowboy actor who also did the voice-overs for the Francis television programs.

So what was the basis of Francis and his popularity?

Well, the story featured a humorous mule who could think and talk just like one of us, only he was better at reasoning than most, if not all, of his human pals. And what's more, they knew it, or learned it the hard way.

The story grew out of combat tales, anecdotes ("meaner than an Army mule") swapped around by soldiers on the various fronts of the two world wars. Mules were used to transport all manner of military equipment, and they worked side by side with their two-legged counterparts, and they never complained as much as the average Joes, or so the story went.

Underneath these sort of grudging jokes was really an underpinning of deep respect. Mules hunkered down with humans under fire and were often braver—not dumber—than the best of soldiers. Without the mule's backbone and his ability to maneuver in mud and mire, the typical GI would've fought a very different war.

Moreover, there was always the sneaking suspicion that the mule "played stupid to keep from being smart." This was where the humorous myths popped up—mules that were the butt of many jokes were allegorical figures straight from Aesop. The combat mule revealed the lethargy, weakness, foolishness, and vanity of the human kind. And by serving humanity, the mule showed us the real meaning of inanity. He held up the mirror, and we took a good look, and what we saw made us laugh: We were the ass, as it were.

Then there was Francis, who was one "darn smart mule." Francis taught us how to think—without presumption—which, most agree, is not a very small order. His role as an ethical, moral mule got him fame and stardom, and in the 1950s, treatment as an icon. There were seven Francis films from 1949 to 1956. Donald O'Connor starred in the first six and Mickey Rooney in the final one. As we have already mentioned, Chill Wills was the voice of Francis, but the great and gentle humorist Will Rogers was his trainer (along with Les Hilton, who later became Mr. Ed's trainer).

One interesting thing about the surefootedness and uncanny perception of mules is that some experts, J. Frank Dobie among them, believe that horses and mules avoid holes and unfamiliar objects at night by smelling them. This is contrary to the opinion that equines rely only on their extraordinary night vision. According to Dobie, a South American horseman observed a lead pack mule smelling his way along at night. Dobie says, "I have seen a Mexican mule in the Sierra Madre do the same thing and have watched horses both ridden and loose test boggy ground with their noses."

There's an old maxim that goes "Horses stumble, mules grumble but never bumble." For more than one hundred years, in fact, mules have taken people safely down the precipitous trails of the Grand Canyon—and with seldom a loss of life.

Presently female mule wranglers make up more than half of the guides at the canyon, and before the turn of the century, a prospector's daughter, Edith Bass, was the first woman to guide dudes down into the canyon on muleback. Indeed, she rode her own mule from up top to Shinumo Camp when she was only three years old. By the time she was thirteen, she could wrangle a mule better than most cowboys.

In addition to the mule's sure footedness on these slicky, tricky canyon ledges, the animal is also possessed of a dowsing ability—he can find water where it isn't apparent; the burro can do this, too.

Mules are unusually resilient in bizarre circumstances. They can be fed nearly anything. This makes them far more adaptable than horses. In *The Mustangs,* J. Frank Dobie wrote of some mules that couldn't get any grass or hay in an 1866 Montana blizzard. Rather than starve, they sought and ate flesh.

After the blizzard had spent its force, two men, Alexander Topene and J. J. Mann, set out to ride to Helena, five hundred miles away. They found frozen carcasses of buffalo lying in the snow in many places. "Every night," Topence reported, "we would take a hind quarter of buffalo meat and hang it up in a tree by means of a long pole and build a good fire under it, and roast it as well as we could, and when it was done we would lay it on the ground before the mules.

They would set one foot on the meat to hold it steady, and start in and tear off big chunks of hot meat and fat with their teeth and chew it just like hay. The two mules would gnaw the meat clean to the bone."

Another Dobie tale involved a mule known as Reliability. He had all the standard features of the perfect mule, just as his name implies. He was tractable and gentle, and he pulled the plow straight and kept himself steady in the harness. But one fall he was turned into a well-watered, bushy pasture for the winter. Come springtime, when the cowboys went looking for Reliability, they couldn't find him. Finally, they spotted him with a red heifer way off in the far pasture, but they were unable to catch him. In the weeks that followed, Reliability proved to be quite uncatchable.

He had found, it seems, his one true love, that little red heifer, and he wasn't about to lose her. Eventually, Reliability was roped and hauled home, but he never worked well again. According to Dobie, "The only tractable slaves are those who have never known and never dreamed of freedom."

The Characteristics of the Mule

Biologically, the mule is the offspring of a donkey and a mare. When you cross a male horse and a female donkey, however, the result is a hinny. Neither mule nor hinny can reproduce, yet the mule is thought to be the superior work animal because he has more of what the old cowboy called "aspiration for the job."

The mule resembles his donkey dad, especially in the extremities. In fact, he has been described as having "a horse's body on a donkey's legs." If you were to look at him from the front, he is all donkey, but from the back the creature is entirely horse.

The mule has long ears set on a long head. Naturally, the tail resembles the little bellpull of the donkey's rather than the horse's free-flowing banner.

Mules are mostly solid in color, but you will find an occasional pinto. The hinny can be any color, although most are gray. Size depends totally on parentage, all the way from miniature (thirty-six inches) to giant (over fifteen hands). The Poitou, considered a giant draft mule, has such large ears that they are carried horizontally.

4

The Literature of the Horse of Africa

"T he Horse of Antar" is a very old story, probably pre-Koranic, as the tale itself suggests. Its origins are Arabic, African, and Moorish, and implicit in the narrative is the highest praise given to any animal on earth. Muhammad called his own mount Ouskob, or "the Torrent," and this word is derived from another Arabic word, *sakab*, "swiftly flowing water." What is prized more highly in a land without rain than water? That a horse should be equated with something so precious expresses the great tribute paid here. Moreover, it is understood from the writings of Muhammad that the horse was cocreated by the angel Gabriel, and thus its messenger status to Heaven is well understood by "true believers." "The Horse of Antar" is more than fifteen hundred years old, and the setting for its telling, one imagines, was under the blazing firmament and perhaps the night before a battle of lances and swords.

The Horse of Antar

So it was that Antar, the greatest warrior the desert has ever known, rode forth and conquered his enemies, one by one, and he drove before him their captured women and their flocks, and he was called great in the land that knew him; and great in the land that knew him not.

One day, however, a horseman rushed out at him from out of a ravine. The man was mounted on a beautiful young horse, black as night and swift as the wind. When Antar saw this incomparable animal, he forgot everything except his desire to have him. The warrior, who now fled from Antar, was a famous horseman named Harith. With a touch of his heels, Harith's mount fled like a cloud, and Antar chased after him until sundown. Finally Antar called to Harith, "Friend or enemy, whichever you choose to be, hold up so that I might speak with you."

Harith answered, "What is it you want, stranger?"

"I see that you are a noble horseman and that you ride a noble mount. I will pledge your safety if you sell him to me."

Harith was amused. "What warrior gives up his mount without a fight?"

Antar said nothing.

Harith continued, "My horse, Abjer, is of the finest lineage. He flies without wings."

"I can see that," Antar agreed. "But you see, evidently, what I do on the battlefield. If you don't sell me your horse, I will have to take him by force."

Harith knew that he was dealing with no common man, and he answered, "I cannot fight you. My horse is young and he does not yet know that dance. Still, with a touch of my spur he could outrun you, and you would never see us again."

"I would pursue you to the end of the earth, and if, then, you went off it, and spilled away into the stars, I would still follow you." Antar said this calmly, and his even-tempered voice neither rose nor fell. Harith heard him and was impressed.

"I am no coward," he said, "but I am afraid lest this horse might receive a blow that would injure him, for, as I said, he is young yet in battle."

Antar smiled and shifted in his saddle, bringing his knee over the pommel and crossing it, as if he were riding camel-fashion, and he said softly, "I see that we are ready now to bargain, and as it is my great wish to buy your horse, rather than steal him, I ask again what it is you want for him. Whatever that is, I shall pay."

Harith said, "Very well. My price is all of the treasure you have wrested from princes and kings—all of it."

Antar looked curiously at the man. "Is that all?"

Harith replied, "I am the loser by this trade—not you."

Antar gave forth a laugh and shifted his leg back into his stirrup. He drew up his rein and whirled in a circle around Harith, who remained moveless as a sun stone. Harith said nothing. But the eyes in his head, shrouded by a cloth, followed the swift circle and the pattering of Antar's horse's hoofs. Little spurts of hot sand smoked up at each prance. Then Antar dismounted; and so did Harith.

"Here is my hand in faith and sincerity," said Antar.

"For all of your booty—people, animals, everything?"

Antar nodded.

Then the two men met and clasped one another, after which Harith fondled his horse Abjer for the last time. Then he took the reins and offered them to Antar, who, in turn, gave his reins to Harith. So that is how Antar, the greatest warrior of the desert, acquired Abjer.

Now, as the grains of sand made their journey under the sun, Antar's heroic deeds were known from Syria to India and from Africa to Byzantium. On the back of Abjer, Antar found his wife, whose name was Abla. After this, he wrote his Seven Golden Poems in gold Arabic script, and these words remain in Mecca.

Toward the end of Antar's time on earth, there was yet one warrior left that he had not vanquished. This man's name was Jezar. He was an archer, a very famous one. As a young man Antar would have bested him on the battlefield. But at the dusk of his days, he had no heart for bloodletting. Instead, he captured this archer and spared his *life. But though Antar let Jezar live, he ordered that the archer's eyes be put out.*

Now, on the day that Antar came to Yemen, word of his arrival came to the ears of Jezar. He called his slave, Nejim, and told him: "Long I have wanted to avenge myself. If it is true that my old enemy, Antar, is camped along the river, maybe I'll be able to pay him back in kind."

And so Jezar and Nejim went to the river's edge and hid in the reeds that grew there.

"Tell me Nejim, what you see on the other side of the river." Nejim said that he saw a great many tents. "Tell me more," said Jezar, anxiously.

"There is one tent that stands out from all the rest."

"How so?"

"The horse tethered before it is the finest my eyes have beheld."

"Abjer!" said Jezar.

Under the cover of darkness, Nejim led Jezar across the river. They walked waist deep through the shallows, and the herons croaked at their coming. Jezar gripped his bow and touched his quiver of poisoned arrows.

When he found the arrow with the keenest point, he notched it on the bowstring. Presently, Antar stood at the opening of his tent. To Abla, his wife, he said, "I feel something. Something strange in the air."

Abla said, "It is wild dogs on the prowl." Then she added, "Come back to bed." But Antar stepped out of the tent and stared at the heavens. There he saw the star horse known as Pegasus. Nearby his own horse neighed nervously and clumped his hoof to show that something was wrong. "Abjer, you feel it, too." Then the arrow of Jezar sprang from its bowstring and struck Antar a wicked blow.

Yet, though he was mortally wounded, Antar got to his feet and walked unsteadily into his tent. Then he collapsed into Abla's arms.

Jezar, who could see none of this, heard it spoken. He ground his teeth in rage. His old enemy was still alive. However, Nejim guided Jezar into the sanctuary of dark reeds, saying, "Antar cannot live long, for I saw your arrow fly true." This he promised his master, but Jezar was not so certain. "*Whatever power stirs in Antar may unleash forces we know nothing about.*" *Then Nejim sought their hidden horses, and the two men disappeared in the darkness.*

Antar told Abla to wear his armor. She nodded. Abla would not weep over her husband's wound. Instead, she told him she would do whatever he wished. Antar smiled weakly. "*When they see the flash of my battle clothes, my assassin and his henchmen will scatter before you like dry leaves.*" *Abla did what Antar commanded. But while she put on his metal breastplate, Antar sighed and was gone from this world.*

Armored and cloaked as her husband, Abla then danced into the dawn on Abjer. And, as the sun came over the dunes, Abla saw black dots on the horizon—tents, thousands of them, the large camp of Jezar, who was already bragging that he had killed Antar with a single arrow.

It happened that three hundred warriors went out to meet Abla, who had a small army of thirty men. Her enemies, close though they were, could not see the litter of white cloth encircled by horseman that contained the dead body of the great leader.

The three hundred drew three steps closer. The many hooves drummed the sand. The creak of armor and leather rose on the wind. Then an old sheik came to Jezar. "*No doubt,*" *he said,* "*we look upon Antar. See that armor? I would know it anywhere. Well, we may outnumber him, but that is no assurance when it comes to battle.*"

Jezar grinned. "*Do you not see it is an imposter?*"

The old sheik stared at the gleaming figure of Antar. He blinked in the bright light. "*Do you really think that someone else would dare to put on Antar's armor?*"

"*My eyes belong to Nejim,*" *said Jezar craftily.*

Nejim said, "*That is no man on the black horse. It is a woman—or perhaps the corpse of Antar. In any event, we have nothing to fear from either of those.*"

Yet the horseman of Jezar were uncertain what to do; they shifted uneasily in their gold and silver saddles. At the same time, Abla was weakening. Her husband's garment was hot to the touch, and it lay like lead on her soft shoulders. She began to shake. Finally, not being able to support it anymore, she dropped Antar's heavy lance. This movement was visible from afar. Nejim saw it first, but there were others, too.

The two armies, one large and one small, remained in force and unmoving, and the sun rose higher toward the zenith, making the sand glow like fire. Worn out, her eyes stinging with sweat, Abla was roasting inside her dead husband's armor. She parted the curtain of golden chain that covered her face—and, for a moment, she could breath freely.

But in the beat of a heart, Nejim caught a glimpse of the whiteness of her face. "That is not Antar," he crowed. "It is his wife, Abla."

"I knew it," rasped Jezar. "Attack!"

There was a great neighing of horses, a flash of swords. The thundering force of Jezar's army swooped down upon the band of thirty. Yet, from under his death shroud, Antar's voice was heard. His terrible war cry, feared throughout the desert, echoed on the dunes.

The coming riders reined in their horses. "It is a trick," said the old sheik. "Antar lives!" He whirled around and retreated while a hundred of his men did the same, disappearing in the ghost smoke of silted dust. Two hundred more wavered upon heat-shimmering shadows, wondering what to do. "Fools!" cried Jezar, when most of them retreated after the dust cloud of the sheik.

Antar, dead though he had been, now rose, feebly. Begging for his armor, he asked Abla to dress him for his final battle. She did this. No one doubted that Antar had risen from the dead—and they honored him with silence. Armored in the circle of his best warriors, he climbed onto the back of Abjer.

Abla, who had done everything that he had told her to do, began to weep. "If you live," she said, "save what life you have for me, not that blind old beggar, Jezar."

"I am no longer to be here," he answered, "but Abla, love, I will always be at your side."

Then he raised his spear, and telling his men to ride the opposite way with Abla, he sent Abjer into a gallop in the direction of the Valley of the Gazelles.

"After him," ordered Jezar, and his hundred followed with the old blind chieftain, his slave Nejim, and his cantering camel in the lead.

For the rest of the day, Antar led them across the pitiless coals of fire, the sands of death; and, as the sun pounded, so, too, did their horses' hooves, and the thin-flowing rivers of sweat rolled off the men and the lather grew thick as bulrush foam on the horses' sinewy sides and flanks, and still Antar rode on and his pursuers got no closer to him, but always remained the same distance apart.

Until, at last, he came to the canyon, the Valley of the Gazelles.

There, utterly spent, he stopped Abjer, walked three steps, and, like a falling tower of sun-smashed steel, collapsed.

This time, and for all earthly time, Antar was dead.

Yet his fine horse was not; Abjer was alive, and, living, was far more dangerous, unridden and with his master fallen, than had he been alive; for the great horse knew what love was, and anger, and vengeance, and now he turned and neighed his own death song, and charged Jezar and his men.

The great stallion, knowing Antar was dead, would yield to no other human hand, fist, or driven lance, but he fairly flew upon the dusk-wind and, darting riderless, outdanced his tired assailants. When, out of exhaustion, a rider fell, he was ground to dust under Abjer's hooves. And so went the battle, stretching from sundown into starry night. Again and again, armor rang and men fell; and Abjer took hooved revenge until the sands were strewn with death and every man was a broken vessel.

In the end, there was only the blind man, crawling like a worm on hands and knees and begging for his useless life. Abjer granted him that, as would have his master had he lived, if only to allow the man's last days to be protracted in pain, for as it was, eyeless, waterless, and unmounted, he would be fortunate to see the sun of midday.

Finally, Abjer returned to the canyon mouth where Antar had fallen, and knowing his friend would not rise again, he kissed him on the face and stood watch until Abla came to unbridle the great horse and set him free. They say that no man dared to ride him and he remained forever the spirit of the valley, saddled only by sun, moon, star, and shadow—Abjer, the horse of Antar.

II

ASIA

5

The Mongol's Mount

MONGOLIAN PONY AND ASIATIC WILD HORSE

The Mongolian pony and the Asiatic wild horse are the archetypes of all equine breeds in Asia. Their stock has endowed Asian horses with great endurance and hardiness, and, indeed, Genghis Khan (1167?–1227) sat atop a Mongolian pony on his far-reaching raids.

The great Khan's military genius has never been equaled. Nor has his horse been topped for sheer guts and glory. This is a mount of indestructible sinew—and it had to be tough, often traveling more than eighty miles each day.

In addition to transport, the Mongolian horse supplied food and fuel for fires.

The average horse soldier's diet on these torturous treks included horseflesh and mare's milk; the latter could be made into koumiss, yogurt, and curd butter.

The horse manure was good for burning in places where no wood was available, in the desert or in the snow. However, the accumulative smell of these unwashed, dung-smelling horse soldiers—if the wind was bearing the right way—was a residual stink that wafted for thirty miles. This foretelling smell gave the Khan's enemies a chance to escape. If the wind blew the other way, however, the enemy would be killed before getting a good sniff. Notably, the great Khan rode hard and fought hard and generally beat his opponents with the sheer power of his assault.

So the Mongolian pony was a warhorse, a provider of nourishment, a beast of burden, and also a part of the complex Mongolian religion, in which the horse was a gift of the sun. To become fully acquainted with the greatness of this somewhat drab-looking equine, one should look at the Khan's favorite sport, horse racing.

The ceremony that prefigured the race is actually still performed today. Called the *julay*, it's a performance in which the ground is doused with mare's milk. The *julay* is common to horse- and cattle-breeding cultures all over Central Asia. It begins in May, August, or September, all of which are the times of renewal.

Marco Polo was the first European explorer to write about the *julay*.

And when he comes to the 28th day of the moon, of the said month of August, the great Kan leaves this city of Shang-tu and this palace each year on this day, and I will immediately tell why.

It is true that for the greater part of the food for this lord, he has a breed of white horses and of mares white as snow without any other color, and they are a vast number, that is there are more than ten thousand white mares. And besides he has a great number of white cows. And the milk of these with cows and mares no one else dares drink of it on that day except only the great Kan and his descendants, that is those who are of the lineage of the empire, that is of the lineage of the great Kan.

Yet it is true that another race of people of that region that are called Horiat can indeed drink of it. And Chingis the great Kan gives them this honor and this great privilege as reward for a very great victory which they won with him to his honor long ago, and they have this preeminence. He wished that they and all their descendants should live and should be fed on the same food on which the great Kan and those of his blood were fed.

And so only these two families live on the said white animals, that is on the milk that is milked from them. . . . And the astrologers and the idolaters have told the great Kan that he must sprinkle some of this milk of these white mares through the air and on the land on the 28th day of the moon of August each year so that all the spirits which go by the air and by land have some of it to drink as they please and the earth and the air and the idols which they worship, so that this charity done to the spirits they may save him all his things, and that all his things may prosper, both men and women, and beasts, and birds, and corn, and all other things that grow on the land.

In Europe, at this same time, men and women celebrated the sun and the moon much like the Khan did. Europeans were in awe of the magic visitant, Nightmare, who was, according to mythologist Robert Graves, a "small mettlesome mare, not more than thirteen hands high, of the breed familiar from the Elgin marbles: cream-colored, clean-limbed, with a long head, bluish eye, flowing mane and tail." A bit of roughish magic on four strong legs, not unlike the Mongolian pony.

Anyway, around the neck of this pony the worshipers hung a thin disk of Wicklow gold. It was in the shape of a crescent moon. The circlet that held it in place was a braid of scarlet and white linen.

So here was a bewitching and bedazzling horse. But she was nonetheless just another manifestation of the White Goddess, or Gaia, also known simply as Mother Earth. The hymn to her power is found in the Celtic ballad called the "Cad Goddeu."

> *Handsome is the yellow horse,*
> *But a hundred times better*
> *Is my cream-colored one*
> *Swift as a sea-mew . . .*

In shape and substance, the iron shoe of the horse still holds this old mythology.

Too, the moon madonna—once known in Egypt as Isis—is also closely tied to the horse. Not surprisingly, the iron horseshoe, placed upward as a moon-crescent, was a talisman that protected against bewitchment.

It also guarded against the evil eye and all other lurking forms of evil. This is why the horseshoe nailed upward over a door is supposed to be for good luck. Actually, it was for life saving, not luck finding. Once hung upward above the door, it asked for the benevolent spirit of the Great Mother to guard all the people inside of the house. And the winged foot of the horse carried this prayer straight to the moon herself.

Conversely, if you turned the iron shoe downward, so that it looked like inverted horns that were piercing the earth, you were inviting bad luck, evil omens, and perhaps even the Devil to darken your door.

Mythologist M. O. Howey speaks of the horns thus:

> It is in this sense that the horns of the altar are referred to in the Bible: "Bind the sacrifice with cords, even unto the horns of the altar" (Psalm 118:27). In Christian churches the corner on the left of the priest when he faces the altar is the gospel horn, and that at his right is the epistle horn, the two united being the means that enable him to stand with confidence before the All-highest—the symbol of the Motherlove of God, the horn of salvation.

Interestingly, the Hopi symbol of brotherhood is the opposing yet interlocked clefts of the horse's hoof. The Navajo horse's hoof blessing looks like a butterfly; it is really a cloven hoofprint. Medicine men have told us that the butterfly was the first deity to put "the flint of life," which makes sparks when the horse runs, into the first horse. Her tracks look like wings, in honor of butterflies, they say.

In 1813, in London, most of the houses in the West End had a horseshoe somewhere near or on the threshold. On Monmouth Street, for example, seventeen iron shoes were once found nailed to different doors—guardians against the old demon, Nightmare.

But what does the word have to do with a female horse?

According to zoologist and author Desmond Morris, *mare* is "from the Anglo-Saxon and means evil spirit or incubus." The incubus demon sat on the chests of sleeping women, often ravishing them in their "agonized slumber."

Morris says the resultant offspring were misshapen. All of this is part of our negative witch lore, and the confusion with the female horse may been underscored by paintings two hundred years ago that showed a sleeping woman with an incubus and a sinister blind horse at the window.

The concept of hag-ridden horses and nocturnal demon horses is also related to the poor quality of stables in former times. Morris believes that early stables were windowless, stagnant, and sickly structures designed to protect the animal from theft but not from illness. Consequently, "After a long night shut up in the stagnant air, with a serious lack of oxygen, the wretched animals were found in the morning to be drained of energy and bathed in sweat. The wickedness of witches was in reality the stupidity of stablemen."

It is in Mongolia, however, that we find the most ardent devotion to horse magic still going strong. The equine race of the khans is practiced today, and it has no Western corollary except in the horse ceremonies of Gypsy culture, which, of course, came from the East, anyway.

In Genghis Khan's time, only stallions were used in the race of the sun. The riders were boys (presumably virgins) between ten and twelve years of age. One adult was permitted in the race, but he was ordained to come in last. He drank his share of koumiss while his mount was anointed with horse's butter.

One of the fine mythological horse poems from this period is called "Praises of the Ten Stallions Taking Part in the Contest and Race of the Festivities Together with the Praise of the Horse Arriving Last."

It sounds almost exactly like a Navajo horse-racing chant or a Beat poem from the San Francisco renaissance days of the 1960s.

> *If you watch it at the time it is coming in the wide-open great plain,*
> *It is coming stirring up dust like a deer on the mountain;*
> *It is coming stepping through the rocky-stony land;*
> *It is coming fast like the rushing of the Empress River.*
> *If you watch it come racing through the vast great plain,*
> *It is coming, strutting like a skillful hawk, flying over the top of the mountains;*
> *If you watch it come crossing the desert plain like a snorting roaring snow lion;*
> *when, hearing the thundering sound of its hooves like the cannon of ten thousand soldiers,*

ministers and nobles come out to look, they see this horse
coming with mane and tail
streaming in the wind, running in the sharp burning sun,
or like a swan flying through the rain, this indeed is the horse
called Courageous Hawk,
watered at the Joso Spring, pastured on the Joi Hill,
having over one hundred acquainted horses, which has not yet
lost manners as a foal . . .

The closure of this chant is an apology: "I have written this text ineptly: thoughtful, wise, judge if there are any mistakes, carefully point them out. . . ."

Humbly, he is saying that the horse and the race are for eternity. Mortals pondering over the fleet beauty of the moment can do little more than whisper to the equine wind.

The Characteristics of the Mongolian Pony and the Asiatic Wild Horse

The heavily built Mongolian stands about twelve to fifteen hands and is beige-brown with a light-colored muzzle and black mane and tail. The most distinctive physical characteristic is a black stripe over the back (the "eel-stripe") and zebralike stripes on the legs. The mane stops between the ears and, curiously, the horse has no forelock. Also, the tail is different from the domestic horse in that the hair starts growing farther down, giving greater protection in a desert sandstorm.

The Mongolian pony has one last major difference from the domestic horse: He has sixty-six chromosomes instead of sixty-four. This primitive quality cannot be watered down in breeding; as soon as it is bred, the chromosomes drop down to sixty-five.

The Mongolian pony's breeding influence covers all of Asia and extends indirectly throughout the world. All Japanese breeds derive from it; so do Chinese, East Indian, and Tibetan. Small in stature, the

Mongolian pony is still a denizen of the Gobi Desert, from which its ancestors came. A larger version of the same horse is bred in the western part of Mongolia. Crossbred equines, with Russian-blooded Don and trotter stock, are faster than the Mongolian pony, but they lack the stamina and the survival instinct of their desert cousin.

The Asiatic wild horse (Przewalski's horse) was the original fore-bear of all modern Mongolian breeds. Rediscovered by Russian explorer Nikolai Przewalski in 1879, the little horse was the same animal upon which, six centuries earlier, Genghis Khan launched his assault on the "civilized" world. However, by the time Przewalski made his discovery and announced it to the West, the horse that had carried the khans to triumph had dwindled to very small numbers. Their diminished grazing grounds were taken over by agriculture, cattle, and human habitation. Wild as its close relative, the zebra, the migratory Przewalski's horse found its natural territory too tame for healthful breeding standards.

Shortly before the turn of the last century, some of these horses—mares and foals—were taken to the Ukraine and a scientific study of them was begun. One foal and one filly were presented to Czar Nicholas II. Subsequently, the filly died and in 1900 two more colts were caught and taken to Moscow. This pair was probably fed by a tame adult mare.

The next large influx of Przewalski's horse was initiated by the duke of Bedford, who also happened to be the chairman of the Zoological Society of London. In addition to keeping an estate of wild animals in Woburn, England, he also commissioned a German animal dealer, Carl Haggenbeck, to obtain the elusive horses so that he could breed them.

Pressure from other collectors also came to bear at this time, and many horses were captured, but few survived. Of the fifty that made it from Mongolia to Europe, only thirteen lived to breed with their own kind. This pitiful situation did not improve in the next one hundred years; the wild Asian horse simply did not submit to captivity. When only three hundred horses were left worldwide, three Dutchmen set up the Foundation for the Preservation and

Protection of the Przewalski Horse. The aims of the foundation were twofold: to stop incorrect inbreeding in zoos, and to reintroduce the horse to the wilds of Mongolia.

By 1990 the foundation had achieved its goal by securing a twenty-four-thousand-acre preserve in Mongolia so that the horses could thrive in their own environment. In addition, existing stock culled from zoos began to breed without pressure of onlookers. By January 1998, sixty or more naturally bred Przewalskis had been reintroduced to the preserve, while zoo and park stock had increased to fourteen hundred horses. The future of the Asiatic wild horse, carrier of the khans, has never looked better.

6

The Zen Ponies

JAPANESE NATIVE HORSES

O f the eight native horse breeds in Japan, each is small enough to be considered a pony. We can see these same animals in the misty tapestries of the sixth century. Japanese archaeologists have unearthed tiny terra-cotta horses from burial mounds that go back to the central Asian people, who went from Korea to Japan around A.D. 300. Sesshu, the Zen Buddhist artist (1420–1506), painted animals that were so real that, according to legend, they came to life. As a boy, Sesshu was bound up as a punishment for drawing instead of meditating. When at last the senior monks had tied him so he could not move, Sesshu wept bitter tears, which turned into paint. With only his fingers free, the boy painted a rat on the floor. No sooner did he complete its whiskers than the rat sprang to life, gnawed Sesshu's bonds, and freed him. Thereafter, the masters allowed Sesshu to draw and paint whenever he wanted to.

One day in Yamaguchi Prefecture, Sesshu painted a horse on the sliding door of a house. Each night the wild mare slipped off the door and trotted through the village. Always she came to a certain vegetable garden where she ate a bellyful of carrots. At first light the farmer found plentiful hoofprints and lots of missing carrots— but no horse in the village was untethered. Moreover, the hoofprints inevitably led to Sesshu's wooden painting. One morning, however, the angry farmer saw something he could not quite believe. In the mouth of the Sesshu horse there were carrot greens. Looking down at the animal's well-drawn hooves, he saw splatters of mud.

Sesshu was called forth and a decision was made. He was asked to paint a halter on the horse, and he did so right away. Then he was told to add a post so that his painted equine would be tethered exactly like a real one. That night, the carrot pilfering stopped.

There is a story about an unknown Japanese artist whose studio was out in the street opposite Omori Station in Tokyo. This painter was born *at* the hour and *in* the year of the horse. And his only goal, he said, was to paint a million horses.

One thousand of the artist's works—all horses—were sold to a single patron in Germany, a man whose fixation with these paintings equaled his passion for murder. The patron was Adolf Hitler. What inspiration, we may well wonder, did the Austrian dictator find in the horses of the spontaneous Japanese street painter? The very thing he lacked as a failed artist and as a person?

Netsuke, which is made from ivory and wood, is Japanese horse art at its highest level—yet it began as a craft. Originally, these one- or two-inch miniatures were not done for display as much as utility. Seventeenth-century merchants of tobacco and medicine carried small pouches with them (kimonos, of course, have no pockets), and the drawstrings for these were tied to the waist. The ivory "horse-toggles" that tied shut the mouth of the pouch were the first net-suke carvings.

The Japanese horse of war was the means by which a clan leader was assured tribal dominance. Early aristocrats owed their rank to the quality of their mount. In the twelfth century, for instance, the role of the horse was clearly defined by the sacred text *The Heiji Monogatari:*

> . . . two fine horses, one white and one black, with high-pommeled saddles, were led forth. Since it was a dark night, he had pine torches raised aloft and looking at the horses, said, "When one goes forth to battle, nothing is so important as one's horse. These are exceptional horses. With these magnificent animals, how could we fail to destroy our foes, however strong they are?"

The power of the equestrian was often secondary to the beauty of the horse, which all by itself could transform an historical event into a mythological one. This was true in ancient Arabia and equally so in medieval Japan. The samurai mount was not large but strong and enduring—a horse that would neither bend in violent battle nor bow under the calamity of bad weather. Heavy-coated and frequently armored, the various breeds came of rough stock. They were warhorses in miniature.

And they were bred to suffer through the blasts of spring wind, the torturous sun of summer, and the lances of wintry rain. In appearance, they were perhaps less lovely than netsuke, less graceful than tapestry. The samurai steed was large-headed, flat-necked, short-legged, and shag-furred. Not beautiful, maybe, but durable.

The fighting horse was indispensable until the sixteenth century, when firearms were invented. Foreign breeds—the Arab, the Turk, and the various strains of Persian—were introduced at around the same time as the demise of the samurai class. So larger horses began to alter the old Mongolian stock and reshape the workmanlike lines of their mountain-and-steppe ancestors.

At the close of the Second World War, the Japanese still revered the horse as a symbol of warfare. When the U.S. occupying army established itself in Tokyo, it was expected that Admiral Nimitz—in pageantry—would ride General Tojo's white horse into the Ginza district of the city to formalize the defeat of Japan. However, Nimitz declined the honor, so the Japanese military powers arranged to have the horse led, riderless, down the avenue as planned.

The Zen poet Basho was a wanderer, a writer, a painter, and, as his journals reveal, a great fan of the horse. Leaving Edo in the spring of 1689, he spent more than two and a half years on the road visiting places that inspired his Zen meditations.

On one such visit, he characterizes the kindness of strangers, an expression one finds frequently in Zen literature—but in that phrase Basho includes his borrowed horse, as well as the farmer who loaned it to him.

Moreover, we see in his writing an animal as valuable as a house, which is being loaned, in trust, to a complete stranger. So, too, does Basho return a small token of his great appreciation without worrying if the horse will reach its intended destination. He writes of his journey:

> A friend was living in the town Kurobane in the province of Nasu. There was a wide expanse of grass-moor, and the town was on the other side of it. I decided to follow a shortcut that ran straight for miles and miles across the moor. I noticed a small village in the distance, but before I reached it rain began to fall and darkness closed in. I put up at a solitary farmer's house for the night, and started again early next morning. As I was plodding through the grass, I noticed a horse grazing by the roadside and a farmer cutting grass with a sickle. I asked him to do me the favor of lending me his horse. The farmer hesitated for a while, but finally, with a touch of sympathy on his face, he said to me, "There are hundreds of crossroads in the grass-moor. A stranger like you can easily go astray. This horse knows the way. You can send him back when he won't go any farther." So I mounted the horse and started off, when two small children came running after me. One of them was a girl named Kasane, which means manifold. I thought her name was somewhat strange but exceptionally beautiful. By and by I came to a small village. I therefore sent back the horse, with a small amount of money tied to the saddle.

Basho's humility and faith is strongly voiced in this entry from *The Narrow Road to the Deep North*. It also offers us an unusual but at the time typical role played by seventeenth-century Japanese horses, offering guidance in the many-pathed wilderness of the Honshu moorlands as well as on the field of battle.

The Characteristics of Japanese Native Horses

All of the native horses of Japan share the same breed characteristics. They stand under fourteen hands and have large heads and big bellies, with manes and tails that are thick and relatively short. The legs are slender; the hooves are hard, rounded, and well shaped. The most common colors are bay, brown, chestnut, roan, and cream—solid and generally unmarked except for the dorsal stripe. The major breeds are the Misaki, the Tokara, the Miyako, the Noma, the Kiso, the Yonaguni, the Hokkaido Washu, and the Taishu.

The Misaki, originating in Miyazaki Prefecture, has been designated a national treasure. This animal first appears in history in 1697, when the Takanabi Clan started a stud farm to perpetuate this tough little horse.

The Tokara, whose numbers decreased during World War II, are found now in parks in the Kagoshima Prefecture. Because of selective breeding efforts, these horses are larger than the original eleven-hand ancestor, and they sometimes reach thirteen hands.

The Miyako was a major form of transportation until as late as 1960 in Miyako Jima. Efforts are being made to restore the breed to its original form (eleven hands), but European influence definitely diluted and enlarged the physical characteristics of the stock. The herd presently consists of only twenty-one animals.

The Noma is the smallest of all native horses, standing ten hands high. In the seventeenth century, Lord Hisamatsu of Matsuyama Han asked local farmers to breed a packhorse that could be used on remote islands. Today there are but forty-seven of these beautiful miniature horses.

The Kiso is a medium-sized horse that was used mainly as a cavalry mount during the sixth century. The Kiso region of the Nagano Prefecture produced 10,000 horses during that time. Presently there are about 117 that are employed as mounts, in processions and festivals.

The Yonaguni was developed in Okinawa, and it is a small (eleven hands) animal for which a very special single-rein bridle was fashioned. There are two herds still running wild on the island of Yonaguni (in the island chain of Okinawa). A yearly roundup keeps the herd healthy with pest removal and inoculation.

The Hokkaido Washu is also known as the Dosanko, a breed descended from various others in the fifteenth century, when the people began to populate Hokkaido. Today there are almost three thousand animals, and most are allowed to roam freely on this island, which has some of the only wide-open grazing areas in Japan. Somewhat larger than the others, this breed stands some thirteen hands high and thrives under severe weather conditions and when there is only sparse vegetation for feeding. They are used for trail riding, pacing, trotting, and also as packhorses.

The Taishu is another horse bred for mountainous country, where it was employed to haul timber and to help in farming. Its calm disposition allowed it to be a favorite among men, women, and children. The horse is midsized in this grouping of small mounts: twelve hands. There are roughly eighty horses in the main herd, which is located in the hilly country of Tsushima, in Nagasaki Prefecture.

7

The Literature of the Horse of Asia

his story was adapted from the Chinese by story-tellers Chih-Yi and Plato Chan, and as they tell us, "The horse in this story lived long before the Hsia Dynasty, which preceded the Shang Dynasty, which preceded the Chou Dynasty, which was a long time ago." In fact, the tale is many thousands of years old, and its survival is entirely the result of a culture that prized oral renditions of ancient history. It is also the product of a culture that once believed very strongly in magic, and particularly the magic of the horse.

The Good Luck Horse

Once, neither yesterday nor today, neither long ago nor just a while ago, there was a boy by the name of Wa Tung. Like his father, Wu Li, who was a rich merchant, he was very lonely. But unlike his father, who played in the world of commerce and met many other players, who did the same, Wa Tung played with no one but himself. So he was, if loneliness can be measured, more lonely and less a part of the world than his father.

There were other differences between the boy and his father, not the least of which was the herd of horses Wu Li owned. These were a great amusement to him; and besides, he could, if he wished, ride on a different horse every morning of the week. Off to work he went on Monday, riding a snow-white mare; on Tuesday he rode a chestnut and on Wednesday a bay, and so on and so forth right through to the end of the week.

Wa Tung would have loved to ride his father's horses, but he was not permitted to do this. Nor did he have a pony of his own. Yet he loved horses more than anything, and he dreamed of them and they haunted his every thought and played in the shadows of his mind when he was talking to himself, or eating by himself, or walking by himself.

In his loneliness, Wa Tung created a stable full of magnificent horses, a different one for each day of the week and each week of the month and each month of the year. And some of these horses were magic and could do marvelous and magnificent things, which included flying, dancing, swimming, playing, and talking.

One day, however, Wa Tung was not content with imagining his vast herd of eligible, ridable, playable, talkable horses. He wanted to make a horse with his own hands. So he got a pair of scissors from his father's stable, the kind that are used to cut manes and tails, and from a piece of old, discarded cloth that was used to cover some hay, he made a cutout of a pretty little, wonderful little horse. And then something unexpected happened—just as Wa Tung was about to name his creation, a teasing breeze took it out of his hands and blew it over the garden wall.

On the other side of that wall lived a wizard, a mage, a man of magic. Few knew anything about him because he kept entirely to himself, but it was known that he could make and unmake spells of any and all kinds, and with regard to these and to whom he cast them, it was anybody's guess.

The wizard's whim was his compass; he did whatever pleased him. Now it so happened that this old and venerable gentleman was contemplating a huge carp that lived under the bridge over his garden pond when Wa Tung's cutout cloth resembling a horse fell like a butterfly into his open palms.

"What is this?" he asked the heavens.

No answer.

The wizard smiled.

He examined the crude, four-footed thing with its raveled head and shagged tail.

"To whom does this horse belong?" he asked the empty air.

No answer.

Yet all the while, Wa Tung peeked through a crack in the crannied wall and saw his plaything in the hands of the mystery man who lived so near and so far from him. Of course, he dared not speak a word.

The truth was, the wizard was clever enough to make a real horse out of a paper one, and so he was equally capable of knowing who had cut the cloth image that had fallen into his hands. Moreover, as his eyes missed nothing, he knew who watched him so intently on the other side of the wall.

"Whoever made this horse," the old man said, chuckling, "must be someone with very little luck." He spoke to the sky, but his words and thoughts were aimed much lower. "Yes," he continued, "an unlucky or perhaps a very lonely little boy . . . or man . . . has made this shambly little animal. Ah, but if this crudity, this oddity, could but talk and paw the air, he would be a sight to see."

Wa Tung, hearing these words, lost his footing on a moss-cased stone and fell with a little grunt. However, the wise mage pretended not to hear him fall, and he went on with his soliloquy to the sun and sky.

"Should the gods be willing to grant through my prayers one small wish, I would make this lifeless horse live so that he might remove loneliness from the world and make people happier. This is not a selfish wish, so I ask that it be granted. . . ." And then with a whisk of his fulsome sleeves, the magician tossed the cloth creature into the sky and it butterflied back over the fence; but when it settled back onto the earth, it

rose up immediately and became a small, sturdy, lively pony that was every bit as real as Wa Tung himself.

The amazed boy let out a gasp of surprise and pleasure. In all his lonely life he had never seen anything like this. His horse, his little, silly cutout horse, was alive! Quickly he went to it and felt all over its grayish body to find a flaw—but there was not one.

The horse was just like he had made it—rough and strong, capable and tough, but not very large. Its mane and tail were undistinguished, and it had a dark line down its back, and everything about it was like that of any other horse, but for one thing—and when Wa Tung saw this, he let out a cry of astonishment.

The horse had no eyes. Wa Tung, in his hurry to cut the creature out of cloth, hadn't made any openings there. So this magical good luck horse was blind.

"It is no matter," the boy exclaimed. "I love you anyway." And he hugged his new friend, and the horse nickered his approval. On the other side of the garden wall, the wizard laughed to himself. We shall see, *he thought,* how all of this turns out. No doubt, it will be of more than little interest, and who knows, maybe it will make the world a bit less dark and people a little less lonely, as I had wished.

Wa Tung could not wait to ride his pony, so he jumped on his back and pulled the horse's mane and kicked him gently in the ribs, and the good luck horse began to walk all about the garden. However, he walked with no regard for anything under his hooves, and he broke pots with flowers in them, and he smashed ceremonial lanterns, vases, and lacquered tables, and in the end, he crashed into Wu Li's lily pond, scaring the ornamental goldfish out of the water and onto the ground. And then the good luck horse did the worst thing of all. Not knowing what to do, he sat on the fish and crushed them.

The good luck horse was seated on his haunches when Wu Li came home. "What has happened to my garden?" he shouted in despair.

Wa Tung stood before his father and hung his head in shame. He knew from his father's anger that someone and something was going to get punished severely. Already he was bracing himself for a bamboo lashing. Tremblingly, he said, "Honorable Father, it is my fault that this has happened."

"You?" questioned Wu Li. "How could one small boy make such wreckage of my serene garden?"

"It was not I alone, Honorable Father."

"You had help in doing this?" Wu Li was astonished. His son never got into trouble—never.

"Do not blame my good luck horse, Honorable Father. For your unworthy son is entirely at fault."

"I see no horse. Why do you make up such a tale?"

Yet before Wa Tung could answer, the wizard on the other side of the garden wall gave his own answer to the unfortunate situation he had created with the flick of his sleeve and the blessing of the gods. "Holy Ones," he whispered to the upper regions of the silken clouds, "bless our foolish blind horse with the ability to undo what he has done."

And no sooner did he say this than the good luck horse, who was well hidden behind a thicket of gold-trunked, ghost-leaved bamboo, stepped out into the sunlight and, walking backward, undid everything he had previously done so badly.

Clop, clop, he went, splashing awkwardly into the lily pond. Swifft, swafft went the dead fish, who were alive again as they dived back into the still-green, tranquil pool. And, as the good luck horse stumbled backward, all the things he had destroyed went back into place, perfect and undisturbed.

When all was as it should be, Wu Li shook his head. "When I heard you call him good luck horse, I decided that if such an animal existed at all, surely he was wrongly named. After seeing my garden and hearing your story, I said to myself, if there is such a horse, I will name him Bad Luck, not Good Luck. But now I see there is really a horse here, though where he sprouted from I do not know, and his luck comes in waves of bad and good. Therefore, since he is real and since he is somehow ours, his name shall be Good Luck Bad Luck Horse. Now, do as I say, Wa Tung: Put this foolish and fitful animal away in the stable and keep him locked up where he belongs."

Bowing and saying "Yes, Honorable Father," Wa Tung did as he was told, but when the unfortunate pony was secured and hobbled, Wa Tung heard a noise that sounded very much like human crying. He looked at his pony and saw that where the animal's eyes should have been there were tears, and the water flowed down the pony's gray-haired face and stained him with sorrowful streaks.

"I see that you just want to be loved," Wa Tung said in sympathy, and he put his head next to his pony's and hugged the little horse hard and said, "Do not worry, tomorrow I will take you out of the stable. Perhaps you were not meant for the world of men but rather the world of the horse."

The next day Wa Tung set Good Luck Bad Luck Horse free to roam the ample fields of his father's pastureland. Curious, the other horses came forward to meet the newcomer, but when they saw he had no eyes, they shuddered and pawed the ground. Some of them kicked him and then all of them scattered like storm clouds, and the air was full of whinnying and the earth resounded with drumming hooves.

Wa Tung's father came out of his study, his face furrowed with wrath. "See what bad luck this horse of yours brings!" he said harshly. "Now my calm herd is nothing but belligerent runaways. This ungainly animal is too ill-mannered to live with us anymore. You must get rid of him, Wa Tung."

Now the poor boy did not know what to do, but he obeyed his father and took the sad little pony to a distant corner of the property and tethered him to a thick mulberry tree and left him there in tears—for, once again, both he and the horse were weeping.

"How much unhappiness can be borne?" whispered the wizard, who watched all of this from afar. "It seems my spell and Heaven's wish are not the same at all but have only confused things terribly. Therefore, I ask of the gods for one more thing—let Good Luck Bad Luck Horse fly, and see. Let him fly away and do as he will, and if he never returns, it will be all right."

That night, when everyone was asleep, Good Luck Bad Luck Horse discovered his tether had fallen off along with his halter and hobbles. Quietly he stole away from the mulberry tree, jumped the garden wall, and found himself flying over peaked houses and hills toward the distant mountains of jade. He flew like a great crane through the clouds and the filtered moonlight, and soon the mountains drew near and there was the Great Wall, and he flew over it with ease.

I have come such a long way in so short a time, *he thought,* and what do I do now that I am in so strange a land? *Then and there he looked down and saw a beautiful mare nibbling the fresh shoots of spring grass on a wind-blown hillock. When she saw Good Luck Bad Luck Horse flying by like a streamer of fog pushed by the breeze, the mare said to herself, "Who is this handsome horse, and where does he come from?"*

No sooner said than Good Luck Bad Luck Horse settled softly onto the ground beside her. She was so lovely, he asked her name, and she replied, "But I asked you first," and he said, "Very well, I shall tell you, but you must promise not to laugh."

She agreed and he said, shyly, "My name is Good Luck Bad Luck Horse." Immediately, the pretty mare chuckled.

"You promised not to laugh," he reminded. He was already sorry that he had told her what he was called. But she only threw back her head and shook her mane and said, "My name is no better. They call me No Good Mare, which is why I am by myself on this empty slope. I have no work, for no one loves a useless thing, which is what I am."

Good Luck Bad Luck Horse let out a little laugh.

"What is so funny?" she wanted to know.

"I thought I was the only one," he said.

She shook her head and her forelock fell about her eyes.

"Maybe we are two of a kind."

"I think so."

So the two stayed with each other on that lonesome hilltop and they enjoyed their solitude and they romped and frisked and were happy together, and in time, they were married. After a while, Good Luck Bad Luck Horse—though he was content in all ways—began to wonder what had become of his friend Wa Tung, and he asked his wife if she would like to visit another place, far away to the south. She said she would love to travel that way, but she added, "I am not able to fly like you."

"That is all right," he said, *"we will trot along together and even if it takes us a long time to get there, we will eventually reach the garden of my friend Wa Tung."*

Well, as you may imagine, much time elapsed while the two sturdy ponies trotted southward—years, in fact, many years. And while it did not show in their faces or their stride, when they at last came to the gate of Wa Tung, Good Luck Bad Luck Horse saw how his friend had changed—he was all grown up, a man!

Right away, though, Wa Tung recognized his wonderful magic pony, and he threw his arms around his neck and hugged him. No Good Mare saw how wonderful Wa Tung was, and she had no need of an introduction, for he understood fully that she was the wife of Good Luck Bad Luck Horse, and he treated them both like royal visitors.

Now it so happened that great things had happened while the two horses lived peacefully on the other side of the Great Wall. A new emperor had come into power, and he had declared war on the nation that lived on the other side of the Great Wall—in fact, the very place where Good Luck Bad Luck Horse had flown to and settled down with his new wife.

And a sad day it was, too, because Wa Tung, all grown now, was wearing the military uniform of a man who was going to a great battle. "I was just now coming to the stable to select my mount," Wa Tung told his horse friends.

However, looking through the crannied garden wall was the old wizard, and he overheard this and said to himself, "Ah, here is my chance to set things right."

Saying a prayer to the heavens and whirling his silken sleeves, he cast a spell of unfathomable goodness upon Good Luck Bad Luck Horse, No Good Mare, and Wa Tung.

As he did so, Wa Tung's father, who was grown old and crooked but no less bitter, spoke harshly. "I see your Bad Luck is back. And who is that with him . . . Rotten Luck? Tell them to go away, we have enough problems in this land without their making them worse."

But Wa Tung paid no attention to his father. He merely mounted his strong little pony, Good Luck Bad Luck Horse, and, holding a lead rope, he led No Good Mare with them. It was a long march to the battlefield, which was just on the other side of the Great Wall, down the mountain and at the edge of the long, blue river that cut between the mountains of jade.

There, Wa Tung saw his army and that of the enemy facing each other on opposite sides of the river. Neither army had yet struck the first blow, but all armaments were ready, and the archers and swordsmen were lined up and set to cross.

Wa Tung dismounted. "I am sorry it has to be this way," he said sadly. "We have just been reunited and now we may part forever. That is the way of war and it is a terrible thing."

Good Luck Bad Luck Horse did not look worried. He flew over the surprised faces of the gathered warriors. Across the river he went, a splendid, soaring creature of light—for as the sun struck him his color changed from drab gray to milk white, and he touched the opposite bank like thistledown.

As soon as Good Luck Bad Luck Horse met the earth, all the horses of the enemy soldiers came up to him with their riders unable to control them. The horses of the enemy were amazed to meet one of their own kind, a horse who had the power of flight.

Good Luck Bad Luck Horse said to them, "Brothers, cousins, friends . . . we are all relations here. I am married to one of yours and all of you are wedded to my strength of purpose, my power. In war, we, more than the humans, suffer the most. We carry them into battle and yet they emerge to tell the tale, while we, poor beasts, die in our fetters on the battlefield. Today, brothers, cousins, friends, we shall not die; we shall live. Moreover, we shall carry our people, these foolish men with bows and swords, so close to one another that they will be unable to fight. Then we will turn them around and take them back to their homes. That is what I have come to say, and that is what we all shall do."

Horses by the thousand heard what Good Luck Bad Horse had to say, and those that could not hear were told; and they passed on his message to every pricked-up, pointed ear until all that were gathered knew what they must do.

And when he soared back across the river on hooves of rainbowed beauty, they watched him and sighed deep in their throats, and when he alighted on the far shore, the many horses behind him marched into the river with their masters pulling against the reins but unable to turn them back.

Then Good Luck Bad Luck Horse made the same speech on his side of the broad river, and all the horses there heard his message and acted upon his command. And so, when the horses of both sides met in the middle of the eddied stream, the archers laid down their bows and the swordsmen sheathed their swords, for it was all they could do to stay on their mounts in the fast-moving current, which threatened to carry them away.

But exactly at the halfway point in the river, there was a white sand-bar, and there the riders met their foes, face to face, and so close neither side could turn from the other, and they were forced to gently mingle; and more and more riders were pushed from the back to the front, and round and round like a maze, the riders were turned and taken this way and that by their horses, who swam with them everywhere but into a position of battle.

Those who still had anger in their hearts tried to draw their swords and loose their arrows, but when they did they were too jammed together to use them, and they broke out laughing at the foolishness and help-lessness of it all. In the end, even the most warlike cavalryman could only laugh and watch as his horse went around in circles under him in the cold, fast water of the great river, which, by the way, was called there-after the River of Peace and Love.

Thus it was that Good Luck Bad Luck Horse won the day and he and Wa Tung and No Good Mare went back to the mansion of Wu Li, who heard the news and put his head in his hands. "I am so happy, my most perfect son, that you are alive, and now I know that there is no such thing as good luck or bad luck. Instead, bad luck is sometimes good luck and good luck is often bad luck and in the end there is really only luck."

"Yes, Honorable Father," Wa Tung added, "but we should not forget magic."

"No, we should not forget magic," whispered a voice beyond the garden wall, but no one heard it but the whisperer himself.

Then Wu Li bowed to Good Luck Bad Luck Horse and, bowing, announced, "From now on you will be known as Luck."

And Luck, the finest horse that ever lived, bowed.

So did Wa Tung and No Good Mare, whose name was changed to Luck's Wife, and who, in time, bore many lucky children, who to this day still grace the hills of gold and the mountains of jade.

III

NORTH AMERICA

8

The Nez Percé Palouse

APPALOOSA

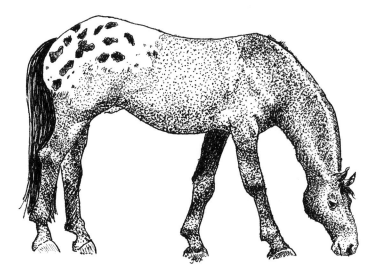

T he Appaloosa is the only horse in America that is a true-blooded stock animal, refined and bred by American Indians. Lewis and Clark admired the horses of the Nez Percé, and according to the turn-of-the-century photographer Edward S. Curtis:

> The explorers spent about two weeks among the Nez Percé on Oro Fino Creek while recuperating from their hardships of their passage across the mountains and constructing canoes for their voyage to the Pacific. They found the people well supplied with horses—herds so plentiful, in fact, that the date of the original acquisition must have been several decades before the beginning of the nineteenth century. One of the chiefs was said to own so many that he was unable to count them.

The hardy trail ponies of the Nez Percé were bred in Oregon and Washington. The first European-American settlers called them *Palouses*, as they came from the Palouse River region of Oregon. In time, "a Palouse horse" was simplified to *a-palouse*, then to *Appaloosa*.

Although the horse was admired by the Americans who traveled through the Nez Percé lands, the Appaloosa seemed doomed right from the start. The Indians were soon going to be reservation-bound, and their horses were rounded up and sold off to the government, which either used them for the cavalry or simply killed them. Thus their numbers dropped tragically.

It would take almost one hundred years to bring back this horse in sufficient numbers for breeding stock. And without the help of well-meaning cowboys, who took it upon themselves to do this, it might never have happened.

In the world at large, the Appaloosa was popular with the Chinese and later on with many European Gypsies. However, the breed goes back as far as 20,000 B.C., and pictographs of spotted horses are found on the fire-smudged walls of caves in Lascaux and Pêche-Merle in France. Characteristically, spots served as camouflage in prehistoric times. The markings have always been popular with people. Horses "speckled, and white" are mentioned in Zechariah 1:8 in the Bible. However, two thousand years before Christ, Appaloosas, or horses very much like them, were bred in southwest Russia. They were also the principal source for breed stock in China and Persia.

Moreover, the East saw something in the spotted horse that was inspirational—in paint, fabric, clay, and stone, as well as in literature, the spotted horse thrived. In the eleventh-century Persian epic *Shah Nameh* by Firdausi, the Appaloosa is "heaven-sent." The heroes of the epic, Rustam and his horse Rakush, are dragon slayers.

What is there about spots that is so attractive?

Sometimes, mythologically, they are ashes. Certainly many American Indian myths support the idea—the fawn got spots by getting too close to the first fire. Sometimes the spots represent the fingerprints of a deity. Overall, they are mystic touches, something special.

Gypsy horses were often spotted. The horse in Romany lore was considered a clean animal and was therefore sacred. Cleanliness, to the Gypsy, was most important; the Central European Rom believed cats were dirty because they licked their genitals with their tongues. Horses were believed to be pure because they did not.

Michael Stewart *(The Time of the Gypsies)* tells just how important the horse really was, and still is, to the Rom. "Comments about the intelligence and good sense of horses were so common that I gave up noting them. Horses were the cleanest animals and would refuse to lie in their dung. They would drink only the purest water direct from the standing tap in the middle of the settlement and eat the cleanest fodder. They were, as the Rom said approvingly, 'fussy' *(kenjeso)*."

There is also the Romany belief that black-spotted horses have knowledge of the dead. Such a horse was said to stop on the road when it came to the place where a Gypsy was buried. Gypsy horses were spirit-sighted and could see ghosts. This differs from the European belief that says dogs and cats are the ones that can see beyond the grave.

No world culture, however, made as much of the spotted horse as did the Nez Percé Indians of North America. Actually, they brought out the spots in this horse by breeding it specifically for this trait. Spotted genes came from Spain and the Arabian-bred horses of the sixteenth century—yet it was the Nez Percé who perfected the spotted pattern and made it what it is today.

In what manner did they manage to do this?

First, rawhide thongs were applied as a kind of tourniquet to the testicles of all "unsound" males. That way, they would not breed haphazardly.

Second, the best studs were given special treatment, and in this way selective breeding was successful.

Interestingly, the Nez Percé did not breed Appaloosas for hunting, as many historians have said. These were, and are, mountain-dwelling people. They didn't hunt buffalo very often. They foraged for food and were collectors and gatherers. Their Appaloosa-breeding program, therefore, was designed for racing and showmanship. It was really a cleverly devised native art form specifically created and enjoyed by this tribe.

Hope Ryden *(America's Last Wild Horses)* says

> It is not surprising after all that upon hearing exciting reports regarding horses, the Nez Percé quickly came to the conclusion that they ought to have some. Around 1740 they pooled the resources of several villages and sent an emissary loaded with goods to Ute territory to trade for some of the strange beasts, although they had no notion how to ride the animal and no near neighbor to teach them.

Marguerite Henry, whose horse books are usually mythological and historical, speaks of the Nez Percé in *Album of Horses.*

> Of all the Indian tribes in Northwest America the Nez Percé were the wisest of horse people. As a squaw sorts berries, they sorted and culled their horses. The poorer ones were traded off or used as pack horses, the gentle aged ones became mounts for

the old people, but the swift ones, the tough and game ones—
these were the buffalo runners and they had no equal. They
could travel the craggy mountains at full gallop. They could
charge into stampeding buffalo and single out one for the kill.
They were built for rough terrain: forefeet turned in so they
could toe dance the narrowest passes; wide heels to make them
sure-footed; thin tails that whisked through the brush and brier
without being caught.

Other tribes painted their horses for war and the chase. But
the Nez Percé horses were painted by nature with a curious
spattering of spots in clay-red or jet black. Some spots were
rounded like polka dots, some irregular as leaves, and some elongated like footprints.

The above text is nicely phrased, but the Nez Percé were salmon
eaters and berry gatherers, and their buffalo-hunting wasn't on any
kind of a regular basis. The great hunt of the buffalo was done by
the dominant plains tribes such as the Sioux, the Crow, and the
Cheyenne, and *they* used Appaloosas traded from the Nez Percé.

After they were reservation-bound, the Nez Percé stopped breeding horses. Tragically, thousands of their pretty, spotted horses were
slaughtered to feed U.S. cavalry troops. This was the close of an era
of unparalleled horsemanship and breeding, a thing unsurpassed on
the Native American continent.

George Catlin, the early-nineteenth-century artist, was one of the
first writers to write about how Native American horsemanship dif-
fered from ours, and his literary observations were often as sharp as
his brush strokes. On one foray in the plains, he saw the unique style
in which mounted Indians met American soldiers, the art of which
surely transcended any known form of military dressage.

In *Letters and Notes on American Indians, 1832–1834*, Catlin writes,

The distance between the two parties was perhaps half a mile,
and that a beautiful and gently sloping prairie over which he
was for the space of a quarter of an hour reining and spurring

his maddened horse and gradually approaching us by tacking to the right and the left, like a vessel beating against the wind. He at length came prancing and leaping along until he met the flag of the regiment, when he leaned his spear for a moment against it, looking the bearer full in the face, then he wheeled his horse, and dashed up to Colonel Dodge with his extended hand, which was instantly grasped and shaken.

The disparity between Catlin's eye-teasing commentary and the known facts about American Indian horsemanship are most curious. In the mid-nineteenth century it was rare indeed to see native riders with spurs. Further, the handshake is also something of a surprise. Exceptions prove the rule, though, and we don't really doubt Catlin's eyesight or his veracity.

It's just that Native American horsemanship was spurless. Tacking left and right, yes; spurring, no. Force of that kind simply was not necessary, as the native rider worked in sync with his horse, mostly using his knees. The following is from *Turtle Island Alphabet*.

The art of riding was something that the Indian took very seriously: to slide and ride around under a horse's neck, to become, as in the Aztec vision, one thing with the horse. Concealing themselves in battle while riding, mounting, and dismounting with deft skill, tribal people regarded these forms of discipline as a pleasure, and it was obvious they surpassed their white foes in the art.

A cavalry officer once met a plains chief to discuss a treaty: the two parties met on horseback. The white men, following the precise format of dressage, came on the rows of well-uniformed soldiers. The chief, seeing this and thinking it quite elementary, sent his warriors out into a revolving pattern of concentric circles that baffled the cavalry with its dizzying complexity.

The plains tribes practiced horse dances; they sang songs and prayers about horses and they had horse games. In the dances of the horse-soldier societies, the men rode during the dance.

Also, the horses were painted, tails tied up as in preparation for war. Hawk or owl feathers were tied to forelock or tail. Sometimes a human scalp hung from the horse's lower jaw. The painted print of a hand on either side of the neck indicated that an enemy on foot had been ridden down.

Before battle, horses were rubbed and blown upon with medicine to ensure invincibility. Among certain plains tribes, horse doctors were devoted to healing just as veterinarians are today. These doctors aided horses injured on the battlefield and on the hunt, and they were always called upon before and after intertribal horse races, which were popular among the tribes.

Incidentally, horse dances are still practiced today by the Cree Indians of Canada and their relations in Montana. According to horseman Joe Rivera, whose brother is a Chippewa-Cree from Rocky Boy, Montana, the dances are done "in front of a kind of Sun Dance Lodge" where there is "a lot of praying and passing the pipe." He says further,

> At some point in the afternoon the group of singers that came down from Canada who know the horse dance songs . . . we would all leave this lodge, and they would sit and kneel in front of the lodge . . . all mostly young men. Of the eight people there, five of them were my nephews, related to me by my brother. When the singers went outside they started singing the Horse Dance Songs. There are two eagle-bone whistlers, a man and a woman. While the horses are dancing, they stand on either side of the teepee, whistling.
>
> The drummers sing and beat the hand drums. There's a center pole, like a Sun Dance Pole, with ribbons on it and at the bottom chokecherries and tobacco and lots of ribbons tied up. (At the end of the ceremony, the dancers take the ribbons and give them away to people to wear around their necks.)
>
> The drumming is sort of a straight beat for half of the time, and they do this sort of round dance beat, and the horses prance

then. They are bareback and ribboned and feathered, and the color of each one is important . . . there's an underwater horse, a land horse, and a flying horse.

Anyway, the young men jump off the horses and hold them by their bridles and then they dance in place. When the beat changes, everyone jumps back on the horses, and they prance around the teepee for five or six circles, and then they stop and the singers sing again. Then the horsemen dance their horses once more.

This dance takes place in the between-time, when the trees bloom and when the leaves fall, after the Sun Dance, in late June or early July. The reason for the Horse Dance—it's anything . . . to celebrate a birthday, give prayers to someone who is ill, to pray for specific dreams.

New Mexico horse breeder Olivia Tsosie writes that there is Native American magic in the mere possession of a horse. She explains that in training a horse, there is a definite style of action and nonaction, an interplay of emotion that is exchanged by rider and mount:

> What magic one might invoke to bind the horse forever, breathing on it, receiving its breath, and learning to know what it would do, as well as how to get it to do what one wanted. A horse can be guided with a stick tapping its shoulder, the pressure of legs, or the connection with a bit or bosal. The Indians used all of these techniques. Lacking the Christian concept of Adam as the dominator of all nature, the Indian would not have used domination as the goal of interaction with horses.

All in all, the Native American did not take the man out of the horse or the horse out of the man; the two worked in simultaneity rather than hesitancy, and they were not afraid of each other. In the vernacular of the cutting-horse cowboy, letting the horse's own timing to rise to the fore is known, as Thomas McGuane points out, as "getting out of the way or, more to the point, letting the cow train the horse."

Not knowing, really, what George Catlin saw—or *thought* he saw—on that Comanche noon in 1834, we're forced to resort to staring at his marvelous paintings; in those images, the Indians never wear spurs.

American settlers appreciated the Appaloosa's stamina as well as his trail-savvy sensibility. For instance, in 1842 Dr. Marcus Whitman and a friend rode two Appaloosa horses from Oregon to Washington, D.C., a distance of about thirty-five hundred miles, to convince Congress that no other country had claim to Oregon. This was the first official cross-country message delivered on Appaloosa-back, and it proved the horse's great endurance and excellent ridability.

Southwestern horse handler and Appaloosa owner Sid Hausman recently interviewed Jean Prescott, whose great-grandfather brought Appaloosa stock to Clarendon, Texas, in 1903. This was another historic occasion for the breed, and Hausman's folk song "Ten Appaloosas" celebrates the revival of the legendary spotted horse in the state of Texas.

TEN APPALOOSAS

I used to break horses and was well renowned
as a top notch bronc stomper for many miles around
I knew north Texas like the back of my mare
because I rode those hills for over twenty years.

I longed to see the northwestern shore
longed to ride horses I'd never rode before
so I lined up some work on a roundup in the spring
riding herd on a caviada, hear the old bell mare ring

Riding ranch to ranch on the trail to Oregon
lots of wild horses in nineteen-oh-one
with bacon, beans, and coffee to last a few days
sleeping under the stars, breaking broncs on the way

but the north wind blew cold, winter hung on
I got to missing that warm Texas sun
so I rolled up my soogan and gathered my gear
bid farewell to Pendleton and saddled my mare

rode into Clarendon March nineteen-oh-three
on main street, the town folk all lined up to see
the drifting cowboy gone two years today
leading ten Appaloosas he got for pay

In *Horse Sense and the Human Heart: What Horses Can Teach Us About Trust, Bonding, Creativity and Spirituality*, Adele von Rüst McCormick and Marlena Deborah McCormick observe, "Whispering to animals, horses in particular, is not just a matter of softening your voice. Whispering, in our experience, is more than a physical act: it is a state of mind. It is whispering with your heart, like another horse softly nickering to its young."

Sometimes whispering is loud—not soft.

Some thirty years ago we watched a farrier named Clarence work with an Appaloosa named Chance. The man was back-bent with a stoop that made him into a kind of human snail—in fact, he was a hunchback.

Clarence had a kind of know-how that no one would dispute, and he'd worked with horses since the turn of the century.

He was not a *whisperer* in the literal, soft-voiced sense. He bellowed at horses but usually not more than once because that was all it took. His high, reedy voice had an unusual pitch and resonance.

The horse he worked with on the day we're writing about was a Roman-nosed, purebred Appaloosa cow pony from Texas, perhaps one of the original Prescott horses. The ungentle, unridable, beautiful gelding was a kicker, a biter, and a roller that had an unexplainable contempt for people.

We watched one summer afternoon as Clarence stooped down to examine Chance's hooves. We drew a breath—we were sure that he was going to be kicked clear across the field. Strangely enough, nothing of the sort happened.

When Chance prepared to kick, Clarence grabbed hold of his flattened left ear, and with remarkable strength and a pincerlike grip, tugged the head down and shouted something none of us could make out. It was a primal yell, which sounded like *Mc-Gumble-farble*.

With his hind foot poised and his flesh quivery, Chance froze. After which, without another wasted breath, Clarence put shoes on him, and later that afternoon, he got up on his back and rode him.

Chance proved himself to be a great trail horse. He could walk along a creek bottom like a cat. He was surefooted and he liked rough terrain. His lovely white and gray spots blended into the aspen-shaded afternoon so that sometimes you almost couldn't see him standing there.

The Characteristics of the Appaloosa

While the reduced numbers of the Appy, as he is commonly called, occurred shortly before the turn of the century, the formation of the Appaloosa Horse Club in Moscow, Idaho, in 1938 increased the stock so that now this horse is the third-largest breed in the world. As best of the cow ponies, he is compact with strong legs that enable him to hop and turn, to curve and whirl with the finest of other Western breeds. The hooves of the Appy are black-and-white striped; they are sound and extremely resilient to the extent that we have seen horses of this breed unshod and still working, something that must hark back to the original hardiness of the mountain-bred genes.

The withers are clearly defined and muscular; the head may or may not be Roman nosed, but it is usually refined. The skin about the nose is mottled, and the sclera of the eye is white, as it is in humans, giving the horse a startling appearance. The tail and mane are wispy—it was a Nez Percé choice to shorten and thin the tail for easy passage between brush and trees.

Most striking, of course, is the Appy's gorgeous coat. There are five recognized patterns of spots. *Frost:* white specks on a dark background; *blanket:* color over hips is white or spotted; *leopard:* white over part or all of the body with dark round spots spattering the light area; *snowflake:* white spotting over the body but predominantly over the hips; and *marbelized:* a mottled pattern over the entire body. Colors can be black and white or bronze and white. It's no wonder that the Appy blends into the natural environment exactly as his native owner and breeder wanted him to do.

9

The Cowboy's Cutting Horse

QUARTER HORSE

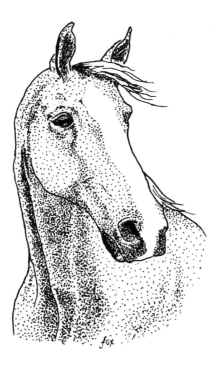

The American quarter horse is the most popular breed in the world. Foundation American quarter horse stock came from Arabian and Barb ancestors, and these were bred in the early 1600s with colonial stock brought from England and Ireland. The fusion produced a heavily muscled, compact horse whose original function was to run short, straight distances.

By the start of the seventeenth century, match races, stacked against fat purses of high-tension betting, became the order of the day, and, in fact, many a lovely Virginia plantation lost its original owner at the track. With westward expansion during the 1800s, the quarter horse, as chosen favorite, went west and in time turned into the American cow pony.

From the very start, a relationship developed between man and animal that was as intrinsic as the horse's love of the chase, the singling out, the staring down, of wayward cows. The point is, men and horses did this thing together, not apart, and for each there was a role to play and a job to do that soared beyond the rigors of work, the selfish needs of either man or beast, single-most and separate.

Horse handler and writer Thomas McGuane has written about this syncopated dynamic in "The Life and Times of Chink's Benjibaby," which appears in the book *Some Horses*.

> Since the days of the trail drives, a horse with the mind and physical ability to sort sick cattle and strays from large herds has had great practical value and is usually ridden by the most accomplished cowman in the outfit. Individual cattle don't want to leave the herd, however admirable the reasons, and they are quick and clever enough to test the horses trying to drive them out. As for the rider, there really isn't time to rein the horse from one spot to another, moving the cattle. Once the cut has been made, it's up to the horse to make the reflexive decisions necessary to drive the cow into the open.

McGuane continues to elaborate on what he calls the "quality of collaboration," a thing so delicate and subtle that it must be watched, ridden, felt to be believed.

A true case of oneness between the human and nonhuman, a state beyond the reach of rationality.

"Human beings," McGuane says, "are species-lonely, relying on needy pushovers like dogs or cats to connect them to the earth's other inhabitants. But you learn something very different from horses who are born wild; and if they're any good, they keep that wildness throughout their lives to one degree or another."

The horse he writes about is a schizoid genius whose work ethic has not been translated into anything as practical as cutting cows. Chink's Benjibaby is much too unreliable to be useful. In one instance of not being fed before the other horses, she drops to the ground, causing her feeder to think she's dead. In fact, she is furious. She threw herself down and held her breath, feigning death, because her status as top horse was not recognized.

Time passes and after her own fashion Chink's gets the message and goes to work her own way:

> She turned around with cattle so quickly that it looked like an optical illusion. And the angle of her body to the ground was so drastic I couldn't see how she ever regained her balance. In fact, she never slipped a foot. I knew from Pat she thrived on impossible conditions like deep mud or slippery hardpan. And she hunted cattle like a cat, deliberately overshooting on her turns, stopping, and watching out of the corner of her eye for the last split second before running, sinking into her dying stop, and catching them up. When the cattle wouldn't try her, she sometimes jumped up and down in frustration.

Chink's brings to mind the oft-repeated advice about bucking horses . . . that you must "ride their rhythm right." To fail to do so brings on another piece of cowboy wisdom: "It's not the short fall, it's the sudden stop at the end."

Troy Fort, a cowboy from Lovington, New Mexico, once remarked of his favorite quarter horse, Baldy: "He runs with his head in your lap and stops so hard he throws you down sometimes. He's thrown me twice, and this year at Houston he threw Skip so hard he nearly broke his jaw when he hit the ground. But I'll put him up against any of them. And with an even break will win. He's the best and the smartest there is."

Once during his career, Baldy was caught in a trailer fire. He was saved but was badly burned, and it was thought he would not work or perform ever again. However, the faithful vet who brought him back to life gave him daily medications and exercise, and his extraordinary care put Baldy back in business. Within a year this remarkable animal was on the circuit once more.

The passion of the quarter horse for work is equal only to the cowboy's prodigious desire to be part horse. Together, the two form an immutable and inseparable unit, but once again the wise words of Tom McGuane: "It is also assumed that the horse does it all. The truth is that the relationship between horse and rider is so intricate that one of the fundamental problems with a cutting-horse rider lies in controlling his own mood. Controlling your mood when a horse turns so sharply as to stick your spur in the ground is occasionally a matter of controlling fear."

McGuane loves animals so much, he says if his dogs were any bigger, he would ride them and have no need of a horse. However, love of horses, he admits, is sacramental and secure.

In the archetypal quarter horse, we have an equine that refuses to be shorn of spirit. Her spirit is her guiding intelligence.

Navajo poet and horseman Jay DeGroat writes of his return to his own culture by riding on the back of his quarter horse. His friend had said to him one day, "You are not one of us any more—you are not mobile," by which he meant that DeGroat had stopped riding; that he was no longer a horseman.

In a rite of passage on a mesa, Jay sees a turquoise horse come out of the sky. He surrenders his spirit to that horse. In so doing, he remembers the five horses of the sun: "They are the albino horse, symbolizing dawn. The blue roan for noon. The red chestnut for sundown. A dark bay for night. A fifth sun horse is coal black—an unchosen and neutral horse reserved for the Sun Father's son when he should visit Him."

Jay told us that he couldn't have experienced this without being so connected to the spirit of his horse.

THE HORSE SONG OF THE NAVAJO

Holy wind blows through his mane,
His mane of rainbows.
My horse's ears are of round corn,
His eyes of stars.
I am wealthy because of him.
I am eternally peaceful.
I stand for my horse.

In his article "Wagons, Horses and Helicopters," film wrangler Sid Hausman tells what it was like trying to get quarter horses into shape for a series of films shot in Santa Fe, New Mexico. The horses always aimed to please, but the wranglers weren't always pleasing with their aim, as this story amply testifies. It also shows the extreme versatility of the cowboy horse that has to do a little bit of everything, including standing firm while the rider ropes a whirlybird.

> In the late sixties I was working as a movie wrangler. Hollywood had discovered Santa Fe was ideal for shooting certain kinds of films and it was, once again, the end of an era in that genre. Anyway, the first film I worked on was *Cheyenne Social Club* with Henry Fonda and Jimmy Stewart. Stewart rode a horse named Pie and he had ridden him in every western he had ever

done. A quarter horse, at 31 Pie still looked like a ten-year-old. Stewart did not look so bad himself and the funny thing was that he had tried to buy Pie all during his career as an actor and the owner-trainer would not sell, but the two of them, Stewart and Pie, were as close as an animal and a man could ever be. Pie had his own special wrangler, a stuntman who had known Charlie Russell and Will Rogers and had plenty of tales to tell, and I stuck close so I could hear as many as possible.

We had between 75 and 100 head of horses and we were training them for teams. There were very few teams around there then, so we spent most days matching up pairs and working them in sandy arroyos south of town. We'd get the teams used to harness, graduate them to pulling logs and then wagons. If we had a runaway, which we had from time to time, we'd circle them in the sand until they tired. The wagons were from the Navajo reservation and it wasn't that long ago that wagons there were a major form of transportation.

Flap with Anthony Quinn was filmed mostly in the area. We had ten strawberry roans, which at first glance looked to be the same horse. In the course of filming, we needed a horse that was at first wild, then broken to ride and would occasionally pull a whiskey bottle out of an actor's pocket, or other stunts of this kind; and the horse you saw in the film was actually all ten horses we trained. One scene called for a cowboy roping a helicopter. Two of these were brought out from Los Angeles, a working one and a wrecked one. The game plan was to rope the copter's tail, cut, and then film the wrecked one. Everything started out fine but soon went to hell in a handbasket. The stunt man made good his throw and caught the tail and his horse acted accordingly, as if the helicopter were a stray, skyborne metal steer, but the rope got tangled in a juniper tree and the copter crashed and we had to summon up another one from back in L.A.

After the movie business quieted down, I was hired locally to drive a surrey in Santa Fe. The only problem was that there was the stop ring at the end of the shaft—the thing that kept the wagon from rolling into the horses was faulty, and so you had to be quick with the foot brake.

One fine sunny afternoon, I was taking three matronly Bostonian ladies on a tour of the Plaza, heading toward the St. Francis cathedral, when an impatient car cut me off. I pulled the lines to stop the team, but I failed to hit the foot brake in time. The surrey clipped the horses in the rear and they burst down the street like a chuck wagon out of the starting gate at the Calgary Stampede. As we raced past the cathedral with me pulling back on the reins, I knew that if I didn't get things under control we were going to end up in the Santa Fe River. I was thankful it was too early in the day for "lowriders," but there was still enough noon traffic to keep my adrenaline flowing. However, my movie wrangling and my youthful confidence got the better of me, and I dove for the middle of the team, in the hope of grabbing the reins—this was the old runaway stage scene we've all seen a million times. This desperate action really spooked the horses, as well as my passengers, but, fortunately, I landed on the wagon tongue and did manage to catch the reins as planned, and as luck would have it, a local rancher saw the whole thing and joined in by helping me stop the stampede. By then we had drawn a good little crowd of onlookers who were hopeful of a second act. I was unable to convince the ladies to continue the tour, so I helped them out of the surrey, put away the horses and called it a day. That was the end of my driving career on the Plaza and the beginning of my musical career.

The Characteristics of the Quarter Horse

The quarter horse evolved from a mixture of the English Thoroughbred and the now extinct Galloway, a pony raised in northern Britain. There was also a little Irish hobby, a breed of pony found in Connemara. The compact, chunky horse that came out of this union stood about fifteen hands high and had massive quarters. The head, however, was small and neat, and the body was longer than the back; the legs are defined as short cannons and hocks set low to the ground. The quarter horse comes in all solid colors. A recent infusion of American Thoroughbred blood has caused the quarters to diminish slightly.

The American Quarter Horse Association, now the largest registry in the world, was founded in the early 1940s. The official distinction of the breed is determined by blooded stock and the confirmation of limited white markings on the face and below the knees. There are thirteen accepted colors: sorrel, bay, black, brown, buckskin, chestnut, dun, red dun, gray, grullo, palomino, red roan, and blue roan. The official gray color might look like white to the average observer, but there are no officially recognized white quarter horses.

10

The Claybank

AMERICAN MUSTANG

There was a time when the Texas plains were spotted with roaming bands of mustangs. These wild animals were on their own, dependent upon their own wiles and speed, plus the canny scrutiny of the stallion that led them.

The enemies of these tough, small horses were many. They included jaguars, bears, wolves, panthers, and, of course, mercurial weather that could freeze them or boil them, by turns. So the sinewy hard-backed mustang had to be ready for anything.

Cowboys still claim that the pattern of the mustang's buck-and-kick was this horse's only defense against predators from above (and below, in the case of snakes)—this, plus his start-up speed and his eye for detail. These and little else kept him from being another pile of sun-sucked bones. He was one smart horse just to stay alive, and this practical wisdom is with him today.

Holling Clancy Holling *(The Book of Cowboys)* tells what happened when a mustang was ambushed by a Texas jaguar:

> The horse went crazy. He forgot any memories of stables, meadows, and haystacks. He remembered only what his ancient ancestors had learned in the long, long ago. Fear drove him to twist, turn, somersault, leap in the air, and come down on that pain in his neck, that clawing, ripping thing that had him helpless. And, just as in the beginning, the wildest buckers had colts, while the weaker ones were turned into horsemeat.

By the same token, the mustang was patient, too. He would stand and wait, if necessary, and not move a muscle until the right moment. In his judgment of men, he grew wiser as time went on. He learned that humans were captors, foes, friends, and fiends. In general, he was wary and full of the very best and the most discriminating horse sense. All in all, he lived up to his Sioux nickname, "divine dog."

Colonial Americans treated the mustang with a heavy hand, however. These men envisioned themselves as knights of old. They rode horses of Spanish stock proudly and recklessly but always prominently, as gentlemen of leisure and influence were supposed to do. The same horse stock in the West, used as cavalry mounts, were little better than tamed-down, saddled-up mustangs; but in the North and South the Spanish-blooded horses were flaunted as thoroughbreds.

George Washington surprised fellow plantation owners by riding his Spanish horse through Indian country alone and undaunted. One hundred years earlier, Sir Walter Raleigh, on first seeing Spanish mounts, said they were the finest horses, beautiful and "strangely wise." His appreciation bordered on religious awe.

Commentaries today reflect that the English-imitation thoroughbred, so-called, was really a Berber horse. Horse authority and Spanish Barb breeder Olivia Tsosie writes, "All Spanish horses are descended from the working horses of the Spanish Empire." This includes the North African Barb, whose name comes from Berber (the Islamic conquerors of Spain) and the Spanish horse, which was the premiere *equus* of Europe for two hundred years, the favored mount of kings and captains.

Naturally, the animals that so awed Sir Walter Raleigh were members of this same blooded stock. Feral herds, loosed on the deserts and plains, were conquistador horses that had broken free—they were called *mestena* by the Spanish, mustangs by the Americans.

The Sioux called them "divine dogs," and it is hard to imagine these Great Plains people without them. Yet just two centuries ago they were a forest people, plodding footmen of the headwaters of the Mississippi, who couldn't compete with their ferocious neighbors, the Chippewa. Pushed out upon the buffalo plains, the Sioux were reborn as a nation on horseback. These once ineffective footmen quickly became the most facile and most dreaded cavalry in the West.

Of all the horses—and myths—worldwide that show the temperament and beauty and longevity of the mustang, there is no animal more famous nor more curious than the horse called Comanche. The fame of Comanche, the only survivor of what is known as Custer's Last Stand, has spread for more than one hundred years. He is the lone equine survivor, the silent hero of the time, the witness of something greater than the tragic physical battle of white and Indian.

If he had miraculously been given the gift of speech, Comanche's worth would be less than what it is today, for it is his muteness that intrigues, and transforms, what we *imagine*—in *this* his greatness is stored for all time.

On the pragmatic matter of ancestry, Comanche is also somewhat indefinable. Some have called him a Morgan cavalry horse, and his weight and bay color fit the Morgan type. But that is true only for those who insist Comanche is a bay. Some believe the color has changed. He has also been known as buckskin, claybank, sorrel, light bay, yellow bay, bay gelding, mouse-colored bay, a Przewalski's horse, and line-back buckskin.

However, these descriptions beg the issue—Comanche is all these things, and more. J. Frank Dobie *(The Mustangs)* says, "Buckskin and claybank are other names for dun." More to the point, clay colors are derived from different geographical places, so it's safe to say that Comanche had a kind of primal tawniness to him, and perhaps we should leave it at that.

Comanche's general description goes something like this: black-tipped ears, a small white patch in the saddle area, a white star on the forehead, a short sock on the left hind foot. He stood about fifteen hands and weighed between 925 and 950 pounds.

Undoubtedly, Comanche was a horse of Spanish blood, but the strange circumstances of his survival have forced him into the guise of a symbolic and surreal being whose mythology is so entangled with Custer's (they were both wearing "buckskin," some authors report) that they have become dual parties of an allegory—players of good and evil, tragedy and comedy, farce and fable.

We think we know the horse; we only imagine we know the man.

And, after more than a century of "fact-finding," each one is still shrouded in misinformation, misapprehension, and equal measures of finely laid false mythology.

The details of the Battle of the Little Bighorn are also, after 124 years, dependent on whose story is being told—American Indian, white American, cavalryman, or Indian horseman.

The likely story, however, is that Comanche stood up in battle just as his ancestors had done for thousands of years; he lived. The bullets and arrows cut the air, and some pierced him, but he stood as he had been trained to do. Many of Custer's mounts were green; few were die-hard warhorses like Comanche. He had seen blood flow and heard bullets whine before. The green mounts bucked and bolted. A lot of them were killed by soldiers to form a barrier in front of the besieged men.

When his rider, Captain Myles Keogh, dropped down and fired his rifle between Comanche's forefeet and under his breast, the enduring animal held stock-still. The same bullet that killed Keogh rent Comanche as well, but with equine battle poise, the horse remained standing.

Legend says that Keogh's hand was fastened on Comanche's rein, and this was why the warriors left the man and his mount untouched. In fact, Keogh *was* left in uniform, his body unmutilated, his crucifix untouched on his neck.

Other myths tell how Comanche galloped toward the Indian attackers, crushing them in his path—or, at the very least, scattering them in all directions. Either way, he was found *after* the Seventh Cavalry was no more. He was there, wandering the corpse-laden hills—or, as some say, down by the river—or, perhaps, as most insist, standing by his fallen rider.

Since all usable cavalry horses were rounded up by the Sioux and Cheyenne and other tribesmen, it is hard to figure why they left Comanche unherded, untaken, alone, and undefiled.

As it was, he stayed on that grisly death field for two whole days before he was found by Custer's reinforcements.

Confusing as all this is, there is less to be gained by trying to learn anything truthful about Comanche's early or even his later life.

Supposedly, he was first an Indian mount—so goes *Tonka*, the Disney fable. Some say he was given the name Comanche because he was rump-shot by an arrow and let out a bloodcurdling, human-sounding yell that was "like a Comanche Indian."

The horse's afterlife is legendary as well, and though he survived until 1891 and the ripe age of thirty-one, he was on display much of the time. His entire being, by then, had crystallized into a cocoon of Custery, lacy, filigree fantasy. Paintings of the time depict him in all ways but as a real horse.

Experts have long held the opinion that Comanche's muteness is glorious. Had he been able to tell what really happened on that fateful day, the whole program of popular speculation would have popped like a pin-stuck balloon.

Unbelievably, the controversy over what really happened still rages. In the 1970s Native Americans objected to the text that ran below Comanche's mounted hooves. The battle was not a "massacre," they said, and rightly so. This was changed, but then there have been outcries over where the horse should be displayed. Some say Montana, where his master went down. Others say Missouri, where Comanche started out.

In 1986 rainwater at the Natural History Museum of the University of Kansas almost destroyed the stuffed horse that had survived the worst that bullets and arrows had to offer. After four months of restoration, a debate went on about whether—since his corpse was originally stuffed with clay—he should be moved again.

His "life expectancy" after restoration? Experts give him some two hundred years of shelf life—providing he is not moved or rained on.

Since no one knows what Comanche is, or was, for certain, we have to rely on what we do know—that he is the most mythologized horse of modern time. He is nothing if not a survivor, nothing if not a hero. Mute to the end, and beyond, he allows us the liberty of filling in the blanks.

What did he really see? With whom did he see it? What were his thoughts, if he had them? Was George Armstrong Custer *ever* a part of them?

Comanche embraces so many unembraceable things—the living and the dead, the tribal and the industrial, the animal and the human, the primordial and the modern. But more than anything, this single survivor presents an ancient paradigm—one that is as old as the sharpened point of steel.

Thomas McGuane recalls (after reading Andrei Makine's *Dreams of My Russian Summers*) there are ". . . images of riderless but completely equipped White Russian cavalry horses, some with sabers swinging from the points at which they were plunged, running wild through a depopulated landscape suggest the fury of human conflict that has surpassed human control."

The guns of the Seventh, more than a century after they were silenced, stun the summer air. The crippled grass bends in silent prayer. So, too, Comanche stands wondering, in museum silence, over the fallen rider, who won't wake up. He is a horse given to a conflict he never sought and from which he never escaped. And after all these debate-fraught, futile years, he alone is the physical embodiment of that crazed, crucial battle that won't let go of our imaginations.

The Characteristics of the American Mustang

The mustang is usually smaller than sixteen hands—generally around fourteen hands. He has a short back and weighs about eight hundred pounds. The color of the coat is often buckskin with a faint line down the center of the back and soft bars on the legs. Other colors are black, gray, roan, white, and paint or pinto. The mane, tail, and lower legs are often black, and the small, neat ears are rimmed with black. Mustang societies in America, in an attempt the preserve the purest stock, promote the idea that the mustang is descended from Spanish Barb and Andalusian blood.

11

The Horse of the Big Lick

TENNESSEE WALKING HORSE

The Tennessee walker certainly fits the bill for one of the smoothest riding horses in America. In the arena riders sometimes demonstrate just how smooth her gait really is by riding around the ring with a crystal glass of sparkling champagne—and not a drop is spilled.

The Tennessee pacer, the precursor to the walker, was consciously bred around the time of the Civil War to travel the valleys of rocky Middle Tennessee terrain. She was also the only mount that could be trusted to walk the rows of cotton without crushing the plants.

In 1886 a cross between the Hambletonian trotter stallion and a Morgan mare produced the first official Tennessee walker sire, Black Allen. This was the horse with a four-beat gait; half-run, half-walk, smooth as silk.

There is some proof that the blood of Baghdad was in the horses of Middle Tennessee, for John Harding's Plantation Record shows that in 1824 there were 89 mares, and in 1825, 103 mares, bred to an Arabian horse. Considering that Middle Tennessee was sparsely settled and without a large number of horses, it's a matter of certainty that Arabian blood runs in the veins of many Tennessee saddle horses today.

Initially, the Tennessee walker, like the Morgan up North, was a utility horse used for farmwork. But she was also employed for family transport, and because she was so good at traversing long distances over unusually rough ground—"and with nary a trip thrown in"—the Tennessee walker was popular with plantation overseers, circuit riders, and huntsmen. In contemporary times, walkers gained celebrity status through Roy Rogers's Trigger. Few people realize that Trigger Jr. was a Tennessee walker, and so was Gene Autry's famous sorrel, Champion.

There were three official Champions for Autry's films, only one of which was a walker. This horse was a dark sorrel with a blaze face and three white stockings on its legs (the right front leg didn't have a stocking). The original Champion died in 1947 and was replaced by Champion Jr. We remember seeing an early sixteen-millimeter home movie of Gene and Champion doing rodeo tricks. The film was black and white with no sound, but Champion stood out marvelously, and you could actually feel the four-beat gait when you watched it. Clearly, this was a walk and not a trot, but the horse could easily slide into the well-known rocking-chair canter, the three-beat, collected gallop.

An early archetype of the Tennessee walker was celebrated in Jimmie Driftwood's famous song "The Tennessee Stud," recently sung by Johnny Cash in the film *Jackie Brown*. Here is the mythic side of the walker, which struts his stuff but is, in the end, the perfect family horse.

THE TENNESSEE STUD

A-long about eighteen and twenty-five
I left Tennessee very much alive.
I never would have made it
Through the Arkansas mud
If I hadn't been a-ridin' on the Tennessee stud.

The Tennessee stud was long and lean
The color of the sun and his eyes were green
He had the nerve and he had the blood
And there never was a horse like the Tennessee stud.

I had some trouble with my sweetheart's pa
One of her brothers was a bad outlaw
I sent her a letter by my uncle Thud
And I rode away on the Tennessee stud.

One day I was riding in a beautiful land
I run smack into an Indian band
They jumped their nags with a whoop and a yell
And away we went like a bat out of Hell.

I circled their camp for a time or two
Just to show them what a Tennessee horse can do

The redskin boys couldn't get my blood
'Cause I was a-ridin' on the Tennessee stud.

I drifted on down to no-man's-land
I crossed the river called the Rio Grande
I raced my horse with the Spaniards bold
'Til I got me a skin full of silver and gold.

Me and a gambler we couldn't agree
We got in a fight over Tennessee
We jerked our guns, he fell with a thud
And I got away on the Tennessee stud.

Well I got as lonesome as a man can be
A-dreamin' of my girl in Tennessee
And the Tennessee stud's green eyes turned blue
'Cause he was a-dreamin' of a sweetheart, too.

I loped on back across Arkansas
And I whupped her brother and I whupped her pa
I found that girl with the golden hair
And she was a-ridin' on a Tennessee mare.

Stirrup to stirrup and side by side
We crossed the mountains and the valleys wide
We came to Big Muddy and we forded the flood
On the Tennessee mare and the Tennessee stud.

Pretty little baby on the cabin floor
And a little horse colt playin' round the door
I love the girl with the golden hair
And the Tennessee stud loves the Tennessee mare.

Horse handler and wrangler Sid Hausman speaks of his Tennessee walker gelding, Cherokee, whose attributes show how well he understood his role as a trail horse. His versatility and sweet temper, his satiny stride and stamina made him Sid Hausman's favorite trail mount. As Hausman says,

> He could easily outdistance all of the other horses, and like my Morgan horse Sven, he learned to go a short ways, stop, look back, and wait until everyone caught up. He was one of the most personable and curious horses I have ever worked with. Whenever I'd fix something in his corral, he would check out all my tools, and generally follow me around and try to help. He liked to *change breath* with me, putting his nose up to mine and breathing into me, as I would then return my breath into him, in the same way that Native American trainers have done for hundreds of years. As long as I would willingly do this, say, ten minutes or more, Cherokee would do it with me—at his, not my own, urging.

One of our favorite Tennessee walker tales is "The Witch's Bridle." This one, like the horse itself, has traveled about the southland, covering ground from West Virginia to Tennessee to northern Florida. Originally, it undoubtedly has Scots-Irish roots.

The way we heard it, there is a farmer who, having fallen asleep in his rocking chair in front of the fire, wakes with a start at the stroke of midnight. In the dim light of the flickering fire, he sees the spectral figures of six hunched-over men digging at something under the hearthstone in front of the fireplace.

These are witch men from Scrag Mountain, and the farmer knows them, or at least has seen them before. But he has no idea what they're doing in his cabin until he sees them draw back the heavy stone and fetch out seven witch bridles. When the men go outside, the farmer follows them; there are six altogether, but they speak of a seventh who is missing.

Now the farmer watches them bridle up some of his own red calves, and then they ride off into the woods, galloping like crazy. The calves, at first, cavort and jump, but the bridle changes them, making them into low-flying mounts, and away they go into the leafy hollows of the mossy night. Wanting to try some of their magic for himself, the farmer slides back the stone and sees the seventh bridle. Outside he bridles and mounts one of his own red calves.

Immediately, the calf bolts as the others have done. And what a ride it is—the farmer never would've believed a common calf could bound like a deer and nearly fly two feet off the ground, then come down and go up again, vaulting through the forest and giving him the ride of his life. Soon they come to the broad path of Coffee Creek. The calf jumps it easily but the bridle slips free from its mouth halfway across. Then the calf drops into the creek and, striking a log, rolls around until it floats off, calling out pitifully for its mother.

Now the farmer is splashing around, trying to save himself—for he is no swimmer. At the same time, down the creek—swept by the strong current—comes a huge oak tree. Floating straight up and passing him like a great green upright island, the tree offers the drowning man sanctuary, and he claws his way up onto the first limb.

Just as he realizes he's safe, and still clutching the seventh bridle in his hand, a long, blue mountain cat drops out of the uppermost leaves of the oak and lands on his back. Swift as can be, this crafty beast slips the seventh bridle into the man's mouth! Forthwith, the farmer finds out what it's like to be the horse and not the rider. Away he goes, using his hands and feet to propel them through the steep, stony night. Mostly, though, he is aloft, swimming as in a dream, pawing the clouds of Scrag Mountain.

Just before dawn the blue mountain cat reins the farmer in and ties him up in front of a cave mouth. Then he goes into the cave and rests for a while. At the same time the farmer considers his plight. As a thinking man, bewitched and bridled, he knows that if he can get the seventh bridle out of his mouth, he'll be free.

So he just spits out the bit, and the bridle comes off. He hadn't expected it to be that easy, but so it is. But just then, out of the cave comes the long, blue cat, yawning. Quickly, the farmer slips the bridle back in place, and the cat climbs sleepily onto the farmer's back.

With surprising speed, the farmer does a barrel roll . . . once around, and now he's the rider, and the cat's bridled. A kick in the cat's ribs, and they're off like the witch's wind.

Over fallen logs and hollow trees, over hardscrabble and river cobble, the cat dances through the predawn light until they come to a farmer's cabin. There he unbridles the cat, which lies down exhausted under a persimmon tree and falls fast asleep as the sun comes up.

With the coming of the sun, the farmer wonders if the seventh bridle still works, so he puts it on his old, lame plow mule.

Then he climbs on its back, and the mule turns into a glossy, softfooted Tennessee walker, starting off as pretty as you please and as smooth as you go, and the horse has stayed that way ever since. And after this the farmer burned the seventh bridle and made an eighth one for his walker, and they say that bridle and that horse are still in use.

The Tennessee walker is much more than a smooth-gaited horse, dream dancer of the cotton rows. Sid Hausman writes of his walker, Cherokee, that

> he took me home at night . . . got me home from parties when I couldn't have done so myself. One time I took a ranch guest on a ride up to Nambe Falls, north of Santa Fe. It had been a good many years since I had taken that trail, and it was touch-and-go most of the way. After lunch we started back and, try as I might, I couldn't pick up the trailhead again. Cherokee remembered the trail we came in on. I gave him his head and he took me home, remembering all the little side trails, as well as the main one. His high-stepping, smooth pace allowed me the comfort of a long, secure ride that had started out in a quandary of *where do we go from here?*

According to zoologist and writer Desmond Morris *(Horsewatching)*, horses, like homing pigeons, "are sensitive to shifts in the earth's magnetic fields. Experiments using artificial magnetic fields reveal that it is easy to disrupt the homing ability by changing the magnetic forces operating on the birds. There is every likelihood that most forms of life enjoy this sensory ability and that it is somehow based on the presence of tiny iron particles in the tissues of animals, which operate, in effect, like tiny magnets. It seems almost certain that horses are employing this same method."

We recall a trail ride in a northeastern woodland region where hundreds of acres lay between the horses we were riding and the barn. Actually, Gerald made a bet with one of his coworkers that he could find his way back to the barn faster than a horse going along one or more of the circuitous trails. His plan was to cut through the hemlock forest, a dense and shadowy domain, and save about five miles of horseback riding. Then, continuing on foot, he planned to get back on a lower trail that went directly to the barn. In practice, everything went awry. In the dark hemlock canopy, he lost the sun and his sense of direction. It took him hours to get back to the original trail where, as his partner had wisely surmised, he would return in frustration. There was his watch-eyed pinto gelding sort of grinning at him. After a thundershower in which Gerald crouched underneath his horse and stayed mostly dry, he let Old Watcheyes have his head and go barnward without human interference. Anyone who has been lost in this way knows the deep comfort—especially in total darkness—of going home on the back of a surefooted equine.

But how well do horses really see at night?

Once again, Desmond Morris has some interesting answers.

> The strangest feature of the horse's eye is its huge size—twice as big as the human eye. It is one of the largest in the entire animal kingdom and amazingly is bigger than the eye of the elephant or the whale. It also possesses a special light-intensifying device—the *tapetum lucidum*—which is a layer that reflects light back onto the retina and makes the horse much better than its rider at seeing in dim light. It also gives the horse's eye a 'glow' similar to the shine of a cat's eyes on dark nights.

In addition to the uncanny sight a horse has, it hears and smells—and remembers these sensory messages—better than human beings do. As animals that have been subjected to thousands of years of predatory danger, they have developed a remarkable alertness; a stallion can smell a mare in heat from up to a half-mile away, for instance. As Morris states, "Aiding him in this feat is the *flehmen* action, in which he inhales deeply, then curls his top lip upward so that it closes off his nostrils. This has the effect of trapping the female-fragrant air inside his nasal cavities and forcing it to circulate deeply there."

Further, the same surreal sensitivity that makes a horse jumpy and skittish is a valuable quality on the dark night trail going home. Engraved in the horse's memory are all the things that teased it or tested its senses. On the return trip, the horse, seeing the things that may have deviled and/or amused it before, remembers the entire pattern of annoyance and pleasure like an olfactory road map all the way home to the barn.

A horse's hearing is no less amazing. Its ears detect low-frequency and high-frequency sounds far better than we do. The shape of the ear and its mobility—180 degrees of movement—enable the horse to pick up noises with an acuteness that is five thousand cycles greater than ours. Moreover, the horse's sixth sense regarding earthquakes and distant storms may not be ESP as much as auditory sensitivity. This is not to exclude the inner powers of the equine, but hearing does play a positive role in seeing/knowing behavior. Says Desmond Morris,

> Many riders thrown by their horses on an afternoon ride have marveled at the way their animals have unerringly found their way back home, over strange terrain, later that night. Such cases may be examples of sensitive hearing—the twisting ear of the animal picking up distant, familiar sounds—or they may be examples of even more extraordinary sensitivity to the "magnetic map" of the home territory.

The Characteristics of the Tennessee Walking Horse

The Tennessee walking horse has a well-formed, pretty head with small, nicely set ears. She has powerful shoulders and hindquarters, a solid neck, and a short muscular back. Standing fifteen to sixteen hands and weighing nine hundred to twelve hundred pounds, she comes in all colors, and none of these are prohibited by the breed association. The nontraditional colors, such as palomino, pinto, gray, and champagne, are gathering added interest, although the most common colors are black and bay.

What makes walkers unique is their gait: the flat-footed walk, the running walk, and the canter. The flat-footed walk is a solid, four-beat gait; the canter resembles a three-beat, collected gallop. The running walk, the big lick, is perhaps the best known. The way it works, the horse steps high with her front legs while overstriding and propelling herself forward with her hind legs. Her head follows the beat of the gaits. The ride is smooth and absolutely no-bounce. As one might gather, this horse really doesn't trot; she just glides.

12

The Pale Horse

AMERICAN WHITE AND AMERICAN CREAM DRAFT

He was the mane-swept stallion of the Lone Ranger, and his name was Silver. He was also Phantom, Ghost, and Thunderhead, and the legends of his hooves rang in the distant hills of American myth.

He was supernatural. To the American Indian, the mere sight of him, alone, on an iron-dark butte was a burst of visionary power.

For the Lakota, the white horse meant a message from the spirit world. For the Navajo, a gift of the Sun Father. To the newcomers, the just-arrived Europeans, the white stallion was no less a symbol of greatness, and he embodied the vast and milky prairie, the spirit of the unstoried, untamed land. Little did they know that they had brought the ghost horse with them from Europe. Something of the Old World to temper and soften the New, to make it more familiar and less uncertain.

Washington Irving was the first American writer to speak of the "mystery steed." In 1832 he wrote that there was a wild gray range horse that roamed the banks of the Arkansas River. The trader George Kendall said the same thing—"a horse so fast he could never be caught." The white horse's speed was the stuff of legend, and an elusive white equine was fuel for a fire-crackling, storytelling night.

The theme was later explored by Herman Melville. He wrote of "the White Steed of the Prairies; a magnificent milk-white charger, large-eyed, small-headed, bluff-chested . . . a most imperial, arch-angelic apparition of that unfallen western world."

Pristine and perfect, like the white whale that came later on, the ghost-horse legend gave great hope to settlers for whom the land was strange and unfriendly. The horse, though, they knew from the Old World; he was a part of the American soil, and yet they had known this magic animal in Europe. He/she was Gaia.

Melville, however, touched another familiar note with his reference to religion. St. John, the Beloved, had envisioned Jesus Christ riding on a magnificent horse: "Behold a white horse: and he that sat on him had a bow; and a crown was given unto him: and he went forth conquering, and to conquer" (Revelation 6:2).

Even today we hold hard to the myth of the phantom equine. It is that deeply ingrained. In the 1950s we put many mystic horsemen on his back—these included the Lone Ranger, Hopalong Cassidy, Buffalo Bill Jr., and many others. Modern allegorical westerns have used the image as well. The ghost horse is a large part of Clint Eastwood's mystique in *The High Plains Drifter, Pale Rider*, and the comic satire *Bronco Billy*. Riding tall on a tall, blanched horse is the equivalent of invoking these words from Revelation—"And behold there cometh a pale horse . . ."

In northern New Mexico one still hears the old legend, "Jesus on Horseback," the healer with white hair and yellow beard who rides out of the sun or out of a blazing star. Wherever he goes on his snowy horse, he heals the sick like Cabeza de Vaca, the conquistador-turned-saint who lived four hundred years ago.

When we first heard this story in the 1960s, Hispanics in Santa Fe and Taos said the healer sat astride a pale horse some twenty hands high. He kept a little bag of *cachana* root, the fever remedy known also as "blazing star."

No doubt, this myth combines the personae of Jesus of Nazareth, Cabeza de Vaca, and a number of Native American shamans. The latter include medicine men like Wovoka, the charismatic Paiute who led the Ghost Dance movement, and Handsome Lake of the Iroquois, whose Christian teachings came straight from the Bible.

The healer on horseback is such a potent image that many modern writers have exploited it in one way or another. Pulitzer Prize–winning playwright William Saroyan presented the pale equine in his Armenian American fable *The Summer of the Beautiful White Horse*.

> One day back there in the good old days when I was nine and the world was full of every imaginable kind of magnificence, and life was still a delightful and mysterious dream, my cousin Mourad, who was considered crazy by everybody who knew

him except me, came to my house at four in the morning and woke me up by tapping on the window of my room.

I jumped out of bed and looked out the window.

I couldn't believe what I saw.

It wasn't morning yet, but it was summer and with daybreak not many minutes around the corner of the world it was light enough for me to know I wasn't dreaming.

My cousin Mourad was sitting on a beautiful white horse.

Saroyan's son Aram recently wrote, "If there is another single page of prose that better evokes the wonder and mystery of childhood, I would love to know about it." That, truly, is the crux of it—the sense of being a child again in the warm unfolding of dawn and seeing but not quite believing the milk-white wonderful horse that, finally, when we touch it, mount its back, and ride it, reassures us that we are not dreaming, that life *itself* is the dream.

In *American Horseman*, Audrey Pavia writes that good guys on white horses have come to represent "justice, honor, and the American way." She adds, "Perhaps that is why, to this day, people find white horses to be so special. Or maybe it's just the fact that white horses, uncommon as they are, stand out in a crowd. When you see these creatures, with their milky coats, contrasting eyes, and pink skin, you can't help but notice an almost mystical quality to them."

Nineteenth-century Arab writer Emir Abd-Kader once said of the white Arabian horse,

> *In the sun he melts like butter:*
> *In the rain he melts like salt.*

Mythologist M. O. Howey reminds us that in ancient times, the Romans conquered their foes at the Battle of Lake Regillus. Mounted on two white horses, the champions rode triumphantly to the forum at the fountain of Inturna, where their steeds were watered.

Even if you do not know what this is about, it sounds good, it has the ring of righteousness in it. In fact, it stuck fast to the history books for just that reason.

In the Greek myth of Phaeton, the Sun grants his son any wish he wants, but selfish Phaeton wants to drive his father's chariot, which is drawn by tempestuous and fiery horses. The Sun Father reluctantly agrees. Yet the rash boy is no match for the fabulous white chargers that run wild, setting ablaze both heaven and earth.

In the Navajo version of the same story, the Sun's son rides his sun horse successfully: "Today I ride upon his broad back; tomorrow he will belong to another." The communal, tribal ending is more egalitarian, though perhaps less dramatic, than the Greek version of mass destruction and ruin.

In each story, vanity is a youthful frailty that must be overcome by wisdom and maturity. The white horse is a spirit that grows unruly in the hands of the untried. Symbolically, only a seasoned master can ride the wind.

Napoléon had three white horses, but his favorite was Marengo, the Arabian. Marengo is the small, high-spirited charger shown in many paintings of the Little General, carrying him to victories at Austerlitz, Jena, and Wagram.

After Napoléon was exiled to Elba, however, he took several of his horses with him. Yet he left Marengo in Paris, thinking that he'd return for him. He did, too. He rode Marengo again in his final battle, Waterloo, where the stallion was wounded in the left hip. During Napoléon's famous retreat, Marengo lagged behind and was captured by the British. After this Marengo was owned by General J. J. Angerstein, who used him at stud.

Marengo outlived Napoléon by eight years, dying in 1831 at the age of thiry-eight—quite old for a horse that had so much violent human history in him. Thanks for his service came after he died. His skeleton was mounted as a military trophy at Whitehall in London, and a snuffbox was made out of one of his hooves.

■   ■   ■

Some historians say that the horse named Isham was Buffalo Bill Cody's favorite white mount. When the Wild West Show went bankrupt in 1910, a wealthy friend bought Isham and gave him back to the old buffalo hunter as a gift.

Actually, Buffalo Bill owned a lot of white show horses. The one present at his 1917 funeral was a livery-stable loaner that didn't belong to him at all but was just sort of standing in to balance out the final ledger.

Despite Buffalo Bill's affection for Isham, it was the Kentucky-bred, dark half-Thoroughbred named Old Charlie that he loved the most.

Mark Twain wrote a humorous story about this famous horse, and he made Charlie the author of it.

> I am his favorite horse out of dozens. . . . I have carried him 81 miles between nightfall and sunrise, and I am good for fifty . . . all the time. I am not large but I am built on a business basis. I have carried him thousands and thousands of miles on scout duty for the army, and there's not a gorge, nor a pass nor a valley nor a fort, nor a trading post nor a buffalo range in the whole sweep of the Rocky Mountains and the Great Plains that we don't know.

The horses of Buffalo Bill were excellent listeners. They *had* to be, for their lives depended on it. The life of a performance horse might not *seem* dangerous, but in the days of Buffalo Bill it most certainly *was*. The acrobatics and mock battles alone were devastatingly real, and some of the American Indian participants believed, at times, they were having real fights.

A small mistake in the Wild West Show often resulted in a fatal error, just as it can today in the rodeo or touring circuit. Show horses, whether in dressage, circus, or rodeo, have to be the very best of listeners. Their owners and trainers must see to it that everything is in sync. Native American horse trainer Gawani Pony Boy *(Horse Follow Closely)* says that most riders use the widespread method of "telling" to instruct their horse. This, he says, conditions the animal to do what is expected of it—to obey.

Further, he explains, "The problem with telling as communication is that the only two options given for performance are reward and punishment." The horse, in this instance, can obey and be rewarded or disobey and be punished. Telling, therefore, is a very limited means of communication between humans and animals. Add to this the factor of memory, says Pony Boy. "Have you ever raised your hand in anger as if you were about to hit your horse? You may find that in the future just the raising of your hand will cause a shying away."

The reward for obedience, then, is not a reward at all but a fending off of punishment. Pony Boy also speaks of "asking" as a technique, but this, he tells us, can also be a pitfall. When asking, you may also be threatening—and not know it.

Even when asking is innocent, it might run afoul of the rider's deeper wish, to be one with the horse.

How is this oneness to be achieved?

Cochise once advised, "You must speak straight so that your words may go as sunlight to our hearts." But *how*? Gawani Pony Boy says that Native Americans "knew the nature of the medicine dog." They understood that the horse was a herd animal and that its movements were directed subtly by the cooperative nature of the herd as a whole. So the horse is an imitative animal that learns by watching, looking, and thinking—but mostly by obeying the movements of the herd leader.

Pony Boy calls this *Itancan* (leader) and *Waunca* (imitator). And he says that when, as a human, you establish leadership in the proper way, your horse will want to follow your lead naturally.

He cites that a contemporary expedition to the Galápagos Islands revealed that "animals trust humans until they are given a reason not to." Horses, in general, have not trusted humans, easily or forgivingly, over the past five thousand years.

And while dogs and, to a lesser extent, cats have accepted and adapted to human unpredictability and have learned to "work around it," as we say, horses have been a bit shyer about this trust.

To train a horse and to become one with it is a matter of re-creating the level of acceptable trust and to become *Itancan*, wise leader. We can do this, Pony Boy says, by *being*, not by telling, asking, or wishing—just by being. In contrast, one of the cruelest cowboy ways of capturing wild horses at the turn of the century was "creasing," and one of the kindest was "walking." Creasing involved grazing the animal's neck with a bullet so that the horse was stunned long enough for hobbling. According to naturalist Ernest Thompson Seton, creasing did not work well with mustangs because it often broke the horse's neck before the hobble could even be applied. Nonetheless, it was often practiced, and Seton quotes someone as saying, "I seen about a hundred necks broke trying it." The gentlest way of rounding up horses on the range was walking, whereby men simply walked after a herd of wild horses. In Seton's story "The Pacing Mustang" he tells of Jo Calone, a walk-breaker.

> Jo . . . sighted them, and walked his horse quietly 'til so near that they again took alarm and circled away to the south. An hour's trot, not on the trail, but cutting across to where they ought to go, brought Jo again in close sight. Again, he walked quietly toward the herd, and again there was the alarm and flight. And so they passed the afternoon, but circled ever more and more to the south, so that when the sun was low they were, as Jo had expected, not far from Alamosa Arroyo. The band was again close at hand, and Jo, after starting them off, rode to the wagon, while his pard, who had been taking it easy, took up the slow chase on a fresh horse.

For the next few days, Jo and his friend Charlie kept walking their mounts in a great slow circle, working the tension out of the herd, so that on the third day the herd was used to them. On the fourth day, the herd quieted down. On the sixth day the herd was a slow-moving mass of heavy-footed equines.

What a shame that this style of taking horses into a herder's confidence did not become more popular in America. Of course, the reason it didn't is obvious—walking was uneconomical and time-consuming, and given the impatience of the men who tried it, it didn't always work. Perhaps the most amazing thing about roundups in general is that the horses survived at all. By the beginning of the twentieth century there were but a million wild horses left on the range, and by the 1970s the mythical white horse of the plains was as endangered as the Lone Ranger.

In reality, the American white horse is not a breed—rather, it is like the palomino, a color. This coloration is present in the Tennessee walking horse, the Thoroughbred, the Missouri fox trotter, the Arabian, and the Morgan. The American cream draft is not just one of the most beautiful of the white standard horses, but it is the only American draft horse left on the scene. All in all, it is not the breed that captures the eye. It's not even the color. It's the *absence* of color. That and a thousand legends have made the pale horse a talisman, a collective memory that won't go away.

The Characteristics of the American White and the American Cream Draft

The American cream draft horse is an extremely rare breed, with just over two hundred in its registry. According to Betsy Ziebell, secretary of the American Cream Draft Horse Association, "The American Cream Draft is a medium-heavy draft horse of about fifteen to seventeen hands: the ideal (animal) . . . has a medium cream color, a white mane and tail, pink skin, and amber eyes." Many farmers find this animal to be the best small draft for plowing, raking, and haying, and as they are easily trainable and quite docile, they are also used in carriage businesses.

The most visible of all draft teams using this breed is at Colonial Williamsburg, an eighteenth-century historic site in Virginia. There you can readily see what makes this horse so spectacular—tufted-eared, pink-nosed, and sunlight pure, the horse's largeness and largesse is complimented by a strikingly graceful beauty, as if form and function were here married to the world's most benign mythology. The result is kindly greatness, an equine of supernal charm and, who knows, perhaps the very one that Saroyan describes that lucid morning when "the world was full of every imaginable kind of magnificence"—child-light, sunlight, the immaculate light of the white horse.

13

The Curious Colt

MORGAN

I t has been said that "the Morgan horse is one thing; every other kind of horse is something else." And although there is still a lot of controversy about the horse's origins, there is no doubt that all modern Morgans sprang from Figure, the horse owned by Justin Morgan. Morgan was a music teacher, composer, blacksmith, innkeeper, town clerk, penmanship tutor, and lastly, because of a bad debt, horse owner.

The story goes that Morgan got two horses on account, one a gelding and the other a colt. The gelding did not go down in history, but the colt did. It is almost that simple . . . but not quite.

What we know about Justin Morgan's colt is well documented *and* in complete disparity with everything else.

For example, he was variously known to be Dutch, French, Spanish, Canadian, Arab, and Thoroughbred. He was called "a mutant and a genetic sport." One breeder claimed the Morgan was so wonderful, he sprang "full-blown from Zeus's skull."

Because Figure was known by his owner as "my little Dutch Horse," this name stuck deep in the minds of some as warrant-worthy and true.

Did he have Friesian blood, as some insist? His conformation suggests it, but no documentation exists, only hearsay.

Justin Morgan's own advertisement in the *Rutland Herald* speaks of him grandly, and *curiously*, as they put it back then.

> This season at the stable of Samuel Allen, in Williston, and at a stable in Hindsburgh formerly owned by Mr. Munson. He will stand . . . until the 18th of May, then to Hindsburgh, where he will stand one week, then back to Williston; to continue through the season one week in each place. With regard to said horse's beauty, strength, and activity, the subscriber flatters himself the curious will be well satisfied to come and see.
>
> FIGURE sprang from a curious horse owned by Col. Delancey, of New York, but the greatest recommend that I can give him is, he is exceeding sure and gets curious colts.
>
> JUSTIN MORGAN
> WILLISTON, APRIL 30TH, 1795

The truth seems to be that the foal was born in West Springfield, Massachusetts, in 1789 or possibly 1793. His sire was most probably True Briton, a Thoroughbred stallion imported from Great Britain by James Delancey. The dam was a West Springfield Thoroughbred out of the Wildair strain.

Schoolmaster Morgan used him as a saddle horse and, more importantly, as a stud horse, first in West Springfield and later on in Randolph, Vermont, where Morgan moved his family in 1788.

After Justin Morgan died, Figure was hired out to a number of owners, who used him for hauling, plowing, and spreading manure. In his "spare time" he competed in heavy-hauling contests and in saddle and harness races. In these, Justin Morgan's Morgan was eminently successful.

Figure lived to a remarkable old age, considering his heavy use. He lived thirty-two years, always in service, one way or another. Thirteen-plus owners had him altogether, and it is a sad commentary on humankind (*manunkind*, e.e. cummings said) that the gallant little horse that had done so much to improve the lot of Vermonters was treated so poorly during his last years of life.

Legend has it that Figure was not stabled but lived out in the open, unsheltered even in the harsh New England winters. He died as a result of an untreated wound that became infected, but horse historians suggest that his rough treatment, suffering the cold at so late an age, really brought on his death.

Figure, if nothing else, was a primal survivor. He adapted himself to whatever was demanded of him. He was a Morgan to the end.

What makes the Morgan so durable and adaptable is the bloodline that includes both draft and Thoroughbred. Together they make a remarkably strong equine, one whose pulling power is equaled only by swiftness and sagacity on the track. There just aren't many horses that fit this bill so precisely and so endearingly, for the Morgan is also an excellent horse around children. Owners comment he is "downright doglike in the way he follows you all about."

The Morgan's usefulness, as well as down-to-earth prettiness, will always be somewhat of a mystery because of the sketchy ancestry. The funny thing is, a lot of experts refuse the facts—they don't want to agree on what little they do know. So there is still the debate about whether Figure's dam was by the imported Thoroughbred stallion Wildair . . . or whether the sire was True Briton, the racehorse.

Other arguments contend that the stud was a Friesian stallion whose home was in the vicinity of Springfield, Massachusetts. And there is even a wild opinion that Figure was by a Welsh cob stallion. The most exaggerated claim of all is that Figure was a direct descendant of Byerly Turk, which, by the way, would make him Barb and Arab-blooded. Oh, well.

One last interesting argument by Bonnie Hendricks *(The International Encyclopedia of the Horse)* is that since the body type seems to confirm this, the Morgan is actually a descendant of the Canadian horse.

But there is no proof here, only a base of conjectures upon which rests a tower of hypotheses. Perhaps, in the final analysis, we should let the indistinct origins of this horse go and simply be glad that we *have* the Morgan.

Truly, the importance of the Morgan, especially in the equine history of North America, is difficult to overemphasize. It was directly responsible for the Hambletonian trotter and other seminal breeds. Arthur Vernon *(The History and Romance of the Horse)* called the Morgan "the most outstanding harness horse in this hemisphere."

Undoubtedly, he is the all-purpose farm horse of New England. And there is the fact that the Morgan did heavy saddle duty for the United States Cavalry (Vermont Division). In both of these capacities—as farm horse and war mount—the versatile horse received official recognition from the federal government and the state of Vermont. Historically, we can still wonder at how this tough animal could pull stumps all week long and then, on the weekend, win a horse race for his owner. But he did this, and more.

One of the popular legends at the time of Justin Morgan was the story of the farm horse that outwitted and outran the Devil. This myth wasn't new to America, but the prideful colonies claimed it, and Washington Irving later recast it into *The Legend of Sleepy Hollow.*

The spare—but not sparing—lesson of Puritanism is seen in Sam Hart's race against the Devil's black mare. Here is how it goes.

Sam's horse, Betsy, was a Morgan mare that, when she wasn't working on the farm, won every race she was entered in. Betsy was Sam's best friend, and he loved her as much if not more than his wife, Prudence.

Sam was a model citizen except that he thought less of church-going than horse racing. He dreamed of one day building a racetrack, and all day, as he and Betsy plowed, he thought only of winnings, of clinking coins.

One day while Sam was in just such a trance, a stranger rode up to his farm. "I wager my black mare can beat your plow horse," the man said. Of course, Sam's eyebrows went up—he wasn't about to bet money on that day, the Sabbath, but he would, duly appointed, show up on Monday morning any place the stranger wanted to race.

"My name is Nicholson," said the newcomer, "and Monday's fine with me." Sam watched Nicholson trot off on his spirited mare, a lean and fiery horse. But he wasn't much impressed, except for one thing—and that was how Nicholson and his mare *smelled*.

Maybe something is burning way far off in the Woburn hills, Sam thought, for they had come from that direction, and both the man and his mare stank of acrid smoke.

Monday morning Sam and Betsy were waiting at the Commons, where the race was to start; where it ended was at the first cornfield outside of town.

Now, Sam, being boastful, talked up quite a crowd, so that when the stranger came clipping out of the maple woods, a great throng of noisome men, all betting on Sam, raised their voices in a shout. However, seeing the way that black mare was built, they gave some pause for thought, and a few bets swayed back the other way.

In any case, when the scarf fell, the two riders thundered round the Commons and off toward the church. Sam pulled ahead, and then he felt a blast of hot air right behind him. The black mare slid up close like an approaching storm. And to Sam's surprise, he saw Nicholson crouched on his mare's neck, laughing.

He looked again and saw a stream of yellowish smoke come from the man's mouth. Now Sam had an idea who his opponent was, but he couldn't be sure. Then he saw some more smoke leak from Nicholson's nose and he smelled, once again, that awful rancid odor.

"Run, Betsy," Sam cried, "I think it's the Devil himself!"

Three times Betsy carried Sam round the course and past the white church on the knoll, and he stayed in the lead—but barely. Always, there was that pumping, cackling, yellow-smoke-breathing demon, rocking effortlessly at Betsy's flank, as if the race were no race at all but something of a game that, at any moment, could be easily won.

All the while, Sam felt the heat of his opponent breathing down his neck, and it gave him the chills. Finally, not knowing what else to do, he reined Betsy off to the right and went banging up the white church's wooden stairs.

Laughing fitfully, Nicholson pulled off a little to the side. He dared not follow Sam there, and he stayed, hovering sort of, just out of the shadow of the church's tall, white spire.

At last, Nicholson shrugged, and without an argument he dismissed himself and lost the race.

"You win, Sam Hart," he said, flashing a yellow smile. "You've beaten me, fair and square. Not many men can pull that off, I can tell you. What does it matter if you won by cheating? Truth is—well, I have no complaint about that since I cheat myself all the time, so here is my horse for your winnings."

"What about my money?" Sam asked, trembling from the top step of the church.

"My black mare will fetch you more money than you'll ever spend in a lifetime," Nicholson roared.

And in a burst of sulfur-laden fumes, he vanished.

Sam Hart went on, as everyone knows, to become a very rich man. As his adversary had predicted, he won every race he ever entered, and each time he was awarded more money than he could spend.

One day, however, he went to the barn and saw that his wife, Prudence, had taken old Betsy, who was sadly neglected by Sam, for a ride. She never returned. Neither did Betsy.

Sam heard that Prudence was in Salem living with her parents, but he didn't care. Not about the wife or the horse. After all, he was wealthy beyond his means. Moreover, he was tired of racing and gambling—all he did was win, and it was quite boring to him.

After that, Sam turned ugly and mean, and he became the worst drunk the town had ever known. He had money to spare, but he missed his wife and his horse, and his farm, overgrown with neglect, turned to ragweed.

Sam kept to himself. They say he sort of withered away, but anyone who ever saw him heard the same bitter refrain: "I lost my wife and my horse, but I beat the Devil at his own damned race and, by God, he knows it!"

Sam Hart's tractable Morgan, the horse that plows on Friday and races on Saturday, is not unlike the best of the breed even today. Horse handler Sid Hausman speaks of his Morgan, Sven, and a cold ride in a New Mexico canyon where the devil was darkness, quicksand, and fear. He calls his adventure "A Horse to Make Justin Proud."

> While working as the head wrangler for Rancho Encantado in Tesuque, New Mexico, I usually found myself riding on my bay Morgan, Sven, who was my main trail horse. He was good at leading rides and, although he was sometimes a bit too fast, Sven always stopped and let the other horses catch up. I didn't have to tell him to do this; he did it on his own. On this day, he was enjoying the crisp smell of autumn, the new snowfall, and drinking from the icy streams, after which he always quickened his pace up hill.
>
> Sven was born on a Morgan farm near Madison, Wisconsin, but he has been in Santa Fe working as a trail horse since he was four, about eight years now. He is pretty characteristic for the breed, though a little big for a Morgan—some fifteen hands high. He has a wavy, thick black mane and long, full tail and ears that almost look like horns in the dark. Sven is quick to learn

how to open gates and he thrives on having a job, which is not unlike other Morgans that are used today as police horses and on ranches, where they're beginning to compete with quarter horses.

We were taking these folks to a campsite on the other side of the mountain where they could relax and hear Pueblo Indian stories told by Larry Littlebird, the Santa Domingo storyteller. We got to the campsite around five that afternoon; it had already been set up, complete with teepees and a tether line for the horses.

My job was to ride back down the mountain with Paul while Larry was entertaining the guests. We had a truck come up and haul all but Paul's horse and mine back to the ranger's camp. The guests weren't going to ride again until the return trip back to the ranch.

The first part of the ride down was mostly brush-hopping: there wasn't a trail until the mouth of the canyon. Everything went smoothly through the ponderosa paths, long mountain meadows, and small patches of snow until about a mile into the canyon, where we hit a dead tree that had fallen across the trail making it impossible to go any farther—by then it was dark. We had to backtrack about a mile, cross a cattle fence, and go through a beaver pond to get to the trailhead.

In the darkness the hoofbeats sounded louder; sparks flew when iron shoes clipped rocks in the trail. Horses have night vision that is better than a dog and similar to a cat, but I couldn't see much beyond my face. Worse, the ground had gone mushy. I knew there was quicksand around there because Larry had told me of it. Anyone who has ever seen a horse in quicksand knows what a true nightmare is.

Time and again, I urged Sven to follow what I thought was a trail. But he'd just stop until I gave him his head, and then he'd lead us to dry ground. Far off, we saw the light from the ranger's cabin. It seemed displaced because right then we were in the middle of a pond and I was not sure we were going to make it out of there. Sven was way ahead of me, however, and he had his mind set on a dry stall and a feed box full of alfalfa. Fortunately, his will—and not mine—prevailed. True to his breeding, Sven kept his head and used his sure feet to save us from a cold canyon night—or much worse.

There is a touch of mystery in the Morgan, something that does not quite meet the eye—or does it? In her book *Getting in TTouch: Understand and Influence Your Horse's Personality*, Linda Tellington-Jones speaks of meeting the Morgan face-to-face. She gives special consideration to four different Morgans, each with a face and disposition of its own. Looking for characteristics that are dominant, she creates a whole picture from disparate and sometimes misleading parts of the same horse.

About Jester, an eleven-year-old Morgan gelding, she observes:

> This is a horse that is changeable and very complex. On the one hand, he has a slight dish face, which means that under the rider he may be timid or shy at common objects, but on the other hand, the bulge on the moose nose, often a signal of a very strong character and 'herd boss' type, would indicate that he could be very overbearing and domineering with other horses in the pasture, and would most likely pose a challenge to his rider.

She goes on to say that Jester's complex lip and chin shape often indicate a complex character; his jowl shows he is thoughtful, his eye that he is intelligent. From a side view, she says, he seems to be "looking right through you." However, his broad ears show a stabilizing influence. Add all of these things together and you have a complex individual, a horse with good intentions who is at the same time impulsive and somewhat nervous. But, overall, his irrational side is won over by superior intelligence and reason.

Another Morgan that Tellington-Jones face-evaluates is Kennebec Leia, a fourteen-year-old mare: "Looking at her, I find it very easy to believe that horses think; everything about her head indicates her intense interest in the world around her. Refined, clever, curious, mentally quick, and extroverted, Kennebec Leia also shows a strong-willed face, but one that will easily cooperate with another being as intelligent as she."

Many of us see similar things in a horse's face, but few of us are willing to suspend what we *think we know* for what we *imagine we feel* about a horse's true nature, especially when it comes to looking deeply into equine eyes and then studying the shape of the head and facial features.

The Characteristics of the Morgan

The present-day Morgan differs very little from Justin's horse, Figure. Time has done little to change or augment this superlative equine except to pass on the physical and spiritual qualities that make the adaptable Morgan what he/she is. Today every registered Morgan can be traced back to Figure.

The average size of the Morgan is fourteen to fifteen hands. The coats are predominantly chestnut, bay, or brown, although some black, palomino, buckskin, and even a few grays appear sometimes. The deep body, lovely head, and straight, clean legs, combined with courage, good disposition, and hardworking demeanor make the Morgan an American favorite.

14

The Horse of the Hero

PALOMINO

he palomino, that pretty amber horse, is not a breed but rather, like the watermarked shade of a tabby cat, just a color. And though many types of horses bear the golden color, the Palomino Horse Breeders of America represent only the quarter horse, the Tennessee walking horse, the Morgan, the Arabian, and the American saddlebred.

However, the palomino is so much more than a nugget-colored show animal. He was once the preference of Spanish knights and the model for some of the world's greatest artists, among them Botticelli.

Queen Isabella had a special love for the palomino, which was passed down to her headstrong conquistadors. These impassioned, shortsighted, dutiful men, in their mad reach for gold, dumped their golden horses into the sea when a black storm threatened.

Sixteenth-century chronicles tell of the screaming stallions and mares that swam after the ships that abandoned them to the deep, as the seawater streamed through their white manes and they neighed in nearly human pitch to be saved. And we still call them "the horse latitudes," those dire straits, those blue deeps where the Spanish horses drowned.

The first cowboy of the New World had his own golden mount, for, as he reasoned, if he could not be rich in the precious mineral that outshone the sun, he could have his own gilded animal to ride upon. And ride he did, this vaquero—the premier horseman of the Americas.

The royal ledgers of Mexico describe him simply as a vaquero, but he was a *Morisco*, a half-Moor. Visualize him, if you will, a dark man on a flashing, tail-frisking, sun-colored stallion.

He was poor but his caballero blood held centuries of wisdom. His saddlery might contain all that he owned, and the style of his horsemanship, flexible and pliant, was impeccable. He was born to, if not in, the saddle; and that, by the way, was no longer a war saddle with a protective pommel and a cantle like the back of an armchair. It was much less of a load-carrier; naturally, it didn't have to uphold clanky Don Quixote, just a light, little man.

But, anyway, what did the vaquero care, if he did not own the *rancheria* where he worked and sweated and rode under the broiling sun? His overlord, his absentee *jefe*, lived in Mexico City. He had no use for the vaquero or his ways, except that the black man's presence was absolutely necessary to run the ranch.

In exchange for his services, the vaquero became a master without a home, a lord without a castle. In his blood were the caballero, the bullfighter, the Jew, the Moor, the Basque, and the Indian. He was a strange and volatile mixture, the vaquero, but his understanding of the earth and the horse was unsurpassed. In time, and as he moved across the desert to the north, he underwent, perhaps, a small change of skin coloring, but his style remained essentially the same. The vaquero became the very definition of the American cowboy.

If we imagine this same mythical horseman as he rides into the middle of the twentieth century, we see a crinkle-eyed man with a white cowboy hat holding the bridle of that same ancient golden horse that came from Spain.

His unlikely name was Leonard Slye, and he didn't come from the sunburned buttes of Arizona. He hailed from the obscure town of Duck Run, Ohio. True, he planned on becoming a dentist, but fate and a gilded horse had other plans, so the would-be dentist turned into Roy Rogers, and his four-legged partner became "the smartest horse in American movies," the palomino stallion known as Trigger.

The year was 1937 and, in truth, Trigger, who was then called Golden Cloud, was worth more than Roy. His salary under contract was $75 a week working for Republic Pictures; Trigger's net worth was $2,500. That was a lot of money in those days, so Roy bought Trigger on the installment plan, "just like you would a bedroom set."

Years later he was asked about his investment and whether it was a good one. He had, by then, done one hundred pictures with Trigger, and the horse's fan mail alone consisted of hundreds of letters each week, so it wasn't a question he had to think about: "I can tell you for sure and certain that it was the best $2,500 I ever spent."

Perhaps Roy Rogers seems a long shot or a far cry away from the black-skinned vaquero, but actually, both he and Roy are fashioned of sequined mythological trappings. The vaquero wore a wide-brimmed sombrero—so did Roy, but his was rolled up instead of out. The vaquero had a belt with a silver buckle. Roy's gun belt could blind a man with sunglasses.

The vaquero wore leggings to protect against the spines of the cactus. Roy had a pair of *chapperas*, or chaps. The short jacket of the vaquero, the *chaqueta*, worn in the sixteenth century, was high cowpoke fashion of the 1950s, only the new version was snipped out of denim and it bore the label of Levi Strauss. (Roy's comic-relief partner, Pat Buttram, wore the faded jeans in the family.)

But it was the horse and saddle that really bonded these two disparate, historical horsemen. The vaquero's horse, whether palomino or not, had to be an all-terrain equine—nimble on its feet, limber with its rider holding tight, and fast-thinking on all occasions, especially dangerous ones, which were the norm.

In movie after movie, Trigger proved himself to be the ablest animal on the set. As Roy says in an interview,

> They would try a stunt with two or three double horses, and they would all shy away from whatever they were supposed to do. So that's when Billy Witney [the director] would say, "Bring up the old man." He'd always ask me if it was all right, 'cause I didn't want to hurt Trigger, y'know, like when they were rolling barrels downhill behind a truck. Fifty-gallon drums. So we were coming behind it and Trigger'd have to jump those things. They came right at him and he jumped it. But it's a scary thing to watch because that was like my child out there.

Of the saddle, much can be said. The vaquero had no need of a high-crested one, Berber-styled, tooled and fit to hold up a mounted, iron-backed man. It wasn't his idea to sit, tall and rigid, legs straight as sticks. He needed to move about freely and fully in a loose, circular, almost acrobatic style. And his saddle had to accommodate him: It was primarily a work seat, with a strong, steel roping horn and a low, sloping cantle, shaved way down from conquistador days.

The ever-useful, all-purpose horn that had sprouted up front held the vaquero's leather lariat, and the long, oil-tanned leather saddle ties that hung off the saddle were good for carrying all kinds of things. For instance, his *sarape saltillo*, or what got to be known as a poncho.

So the saddle lost its conquistadorian weight and lightened up quite a bit. And it became a thing of great simplistic beauty. Its decorations—conchos and tooling—were shaped by necessity and were neither superfluous nor sentimental but uncommonly beautiful.

The saddle of Roy Rogers was the vaquero saddle updated and made momentous for film audiences—sparkly and pretty, it showed off Trigger's gorgeous good looks, but, if examined closely, the style was not that much changed from the high-horned, low-backed leather saddles of the "late Mexican" vaquero period. The lines are the same, you might say, even if the chassis is a little different.

Roy's saddle was formidable, and its richly tooled, authentically fancy visual appeal boasts triangular silver *conchos* and *tapaderos*, or taps—the leather stirrup hoods that protect the foot from cactus thorns.

There is, incidentally, an amusing story about stirrups that begs retelling here, no matter how random it might seem at the moment.

In 1683 an Austrian baker made a batch of breads for the king of Poland, who, as it happened, was an accomplished horseman. To honor the king, the baker shaped the dough of one particular bread into an uneven circle so that it looked like a stirrup, or a *beugel*. From this great moment in horse history, we got the inimitable bagel!

Back to Roy—only a rich vaquero, or one who had taken a wrong turn as a *bandito* in order to better himself financially, could have afforded such handsome riding gear as Roy Rogers used in his famous appearances.

Today the horse that was once called Golden Cloud is the star attraction of the Roy Rogers and Dale Evans Museum in Victorville, California. Two hundred thousand people see him each year, and, as almost everyone knows, he is mounted in a rearing position, as golden as the day he was cast for *Under Western Stars*.

If he were alive now, Trigger would be sixty-eight years old. However, he died in 1965 at the age of thirty-three. During the twenty-seven years of his stardom, he did much more than ride into the sunset; he brightened children's lives, and even saved some as well.

Trigger was not called the smartest horse in film for no reason. Throughout his life, he went with Roy and his wife, Dale, to hospitals and orphanages, often going up stairs and riding in elevators. When Roy and Dale were suffering from a bad bout of the flu in the hospital in Liverpool, England, Trigger went up seven flights of stairs to deliver flowers and get-well cards.

Rebekah Ferran Witter *(Living with Horsepower!)* writes that "he was often indoors—not necessarily in sawdust-covered arenas—but in lobbies and on theater stages. It was his many indoor appearances that prompted Trigger's most unusual training."

This was acquiring the skill of being potty-trained, something that Rebekah says no other trainer had succeeded in doing, but Roy, with the help of Glenn Randall, perfected it—with, of course, Trigger's great patience and cooperation. Roy believed that almost anything could be done with a horse, providing the handler spent enough time trying to do it: "You practically have to live with them teaching some of those things."

Roy Rogers, more than any other popular movie cowboy, lived and worked and played with his palomino pal, Trigger, the most famous golden horse—and, therefore, modern mythical equine— the silver screen has yet produced.

As children, Gerald and his brother saw the premiere of *The Roy Rogers Show* on the first television set in their neighborhood. TVs in the early fifties were too expensive for most people to have, but there was a family that had a set, and Gerald remembers the day they invited all the kids on the block to see Roy, Dale, Trigger, Buttermilk, Pat Buttram, Bullet, and Nellybelle (the Jeep). The screen was small and the images of Roy and company were fuzzy and phantomlike. But in the bluish-gray fizzle of fast-moving forms, Gerald saw Roy take blows and give blows and saw Trigger rear and neigh and shake his magnificent, white-maned head. It was real, it was unreal, and it was . . . television. Some months later, while those images were still crackling like ghosts in his head, Gerald's father took him and his brother, Sid, to Madison Square Garden to see Roy Rogers in person. On the way they stopped and picked up Gerald and Sid's uncle Willy, a wirehaired, myopic man who loved cigars. The family got as close to the center of the ring as they could, and when Roy rode around the arena on Trigger, shaking hands, everyone crowded in and hung over the railing. Gerald jumped up and was met, midair, by the red-embered end of Uncle Willy's cigar. When Uncle Willy got excited, he waved his arms about, and this time he accidentally snuffed his cigar out on Gerald's right arm. It happened just as Roy rode by, touching the heads of the kids in the first row.

Did Roy actually see Gerald wince and jump, fleeing the sting of his uncle's odious branding iron? He seemed to. Fleetingly, his face froze—"What's wrong, little buckaroo?" And then the moment passed, Roy rode on, and time went about its eternal business of forgetfulness.

The cigar burn would heal, but not too quickly, Gerald hoped, because in that round, core-shaped fusion of seared skin was a permanent brand of memory incarnate—a living moment converted into ineradicable truth.

At school, when he told his friends of the thing that would mark him for life—his meeting of the eyes of Roy Rogers, the King of the Cowboys—his friends made fun of him. He told them they were just jealous, and they laughed all the more.

That night he explained to his father what had happened at school, and his father, folding up the evening edition of the local newspaper, said, "Think nothing of it. No one believed me when I used to say I had met Buffalo Bill at his Wild West Show."

"Did you really meet the great scout and Pony Express rider?"

His father smiled. "The year was nineteen hundred and eight, and

I was eight years old myself. Buffalo Bill rode around the ring and shook hands with every youngster under the big tent, and I took hold of his buckskin glove and he smiled at me and his long white hair hung down over his shoulders, and that's all I remember—just his hand, his smile, his hair, and, of course, his fine, big, white horse."

The next morning at school, Gerald added Buffalo Bill to his Roy Rogers story—to show that it ran in the family—and to prove that he and his father were true participants in American history.

His friends, feeling a little left out, gave him a black eye. After that he kept Roy and Bill under wraps. But every once in a while, even after the cigar scar faded, he would try to tell someone, usually a history buff, what it was like to be a small part of a great event in the world arena of the human heart.

The Characteristics of the Palomino

The palomino, as previously stated, is a horse *color* and not a breed. The gold color is characteristically that of a newly minted fourteen-karat gold coin with variations from light to dark. The skin is gray, black, or brown with no pink spots except on the face or legs. The eyes are black, hazel, or brown. The mane and tail must be white. If there are chestnut hairs visible, there must not be more than 15 percent.

The height will depend on the breed represented, but most palominos stand between fifteen and seventeen hands. The best way to breed the palomino is to cross it with a chestnut. Breeding two palominos often produces a cremello, which is often incorrectly called an albino because—except for the pink eyes—it looks like one.

15

The Literature of the Horse
of North America

The two versions of the Navajo Sun Horse here presented have come from the Navajo artist Joogii (Jay DeGroat), who has retold countless stories to the authors over a thirty-year period. The first story is a part of the "hero tales," or creation stories, of Tobaschischin and Nayenezgani, the brothers who were the children of the Sun Father and Changing Woman, or Mother Earth. The esteem with which the Navajo, who were originally a nomadic culture, regarded the horse is expressed in the apocryphal visit of the warrior twin, Nayenezgani, to his father's House of the Sun. The myth of the great horse Nightway is so similar to Ovid's Phaeton tale in *The Metamor-phoses* that one can easily accept Carl Jung's premise that the human race is one collective unconscious. The second of the two tales concerns a modern Navajo and his own psychic rebirth when he is reunited with the Sun Horse near his home in Crown Point, New Mexico.

This story is Jay DeGroat's personal rite of passage, his transition from an "unhorsed" and "nonmobile" amorphous man living in the white world to a Navajo fully invested with ancient equine, tribal power.

I. The Sun Father's Horse

AN ANCIENT NAVAJO MYTH

In the time of the beginning, when the earth was newly formed, the gods came down from the heavens and made love to mortal women. So it happened that the Sun Father himself had two earth boys, who were called Left-Handed Sun and Right-Handed Sun after their father, of whom they knew nothing except that which came to them in dreams.

Right-Handed Sun was bold and moved like a warrior, and one day, riding on an eagle's back, he ascended to the House of the Sun. There, his father met him and the boy saw that Sun Father had five corrals and five horses, and each was a different color for the different times of day. Yet the horse that excited him the most was Nightway. This was the stallion that his father rode only after nightfall. The horse had a jet mane that was swept back on a long, sleek neck, and his fine coat was agleam with grains of mica.

"This is Nightway," Sun Father said.

"May I ride him, Father?"

"What you want, my son, is dangerous. You ask for a power beyond your strength and years, for Nightway may outrun a comet. He may leap the tail of a shooting star. And, when he comes to earth, he dances on the upper circle of the rainbow. Beware, my son, this horse is not meant for mortals, and I do not want to give you the gift of death. I am proved, therefore, a father by my father's fear."

His warning ended, but no caution was taken by the overeager son, who saw himself riding down to earth on his father's fabulous mount. And so into his eager hands Sun Father gravely gave over the reins of jet. Gently, then, Sun Father stroked Nightway's neck. "Take him back to earth with you," he whispered into the horse's ear. "Take him through the north and through the night until you come to the dawn-land, and there set him down softly, as you would a child."

Then Right-Handed Sun leaped onto Nightway's back, and the powerful horse thrust off into the starry abyss. The excited boy had no time to say good-bye to his father, for Nightway took the bridle made of forged meteors in his teeth, bit down, and pulled the helpless boy to the back of his thrusting head. The reins slipped out of Right-Handed Sun's hand, and as he listed to one side of the heavy-necked horse, he lost all control.

Now Nightway felt the full run of his freedom. His legs leaped wide to the rhythm of his hooves as they rang on the moonlit cobbles of the stars. In reckless abandon, the surging horse took the midnight sky; his smoke-plumed nostrils flared and his tail flashed as he parted the star grass, his hooves of flint tearing up the velvet road of darkness. Far now from his father's house, the frantic boy tried to grasp the flapping, flinging jetted reins. If only I might seize them, he thought, then all might not be lost—but if I can't . . .

And the hooves danced sparks and the long mane drank the darkness and made a song as it flew. Far below, Right-Handed Sun saw the dawn-flushed land, and he grew pale, his knees knocking against the soaked plates of the massive runaway horse. His hair burned at his ears as he and the horse fell through the vapor-trailing night into the spreading rose-tinted dawn.

Now the jeweled stars splintered off, arcing and spinning, and night was indeed dying as they fell, the stars themselves expiring. The morning was coming on as fast as they were falling—the rosy dawn blotting the night-frozen stars—and below, the day reddened; the moon's crescent went pale; sky and earth were suffused in the strain of the wild blood-rose morning. And still they plummeted out of control.

The dawn was amply aglow, and the shadows of night were all but gone. Nightway cut through the peach-colored clouds, pawing, breaking free, still falling. Then Right-Handed Sun made one last try to take the reins, and reaching out, he managed to somehow catch one, then two. Holding both, he reined as hard as he could, not the little pull of a mortal but the goodly grip of a god.

And he felt as a result the double buck of the braking horse. They went into a sidelong lurch that crashed horse and rider into the white-walled meadow of the cloudbank.

The great horse turned to the left, skidding against peaks and pinnacles, mounds and mountains, crags of cloud-mist; and then to the right, plowing through the peach-blown desert dawn, making a splendor of thunder as up came the massive sweat-runneled neck and down came the hammered skull into the shattering cloud plane. Everywhere the pink clover born of clouds spotted the sky in raggy shreds.

Nightway came plunging down, parting the graveled dawn as, finally, momentously, it churned upon the solid earth. His hooves drummed the molten morning, the dust rose up like fountains, and the ridden horse at last bowed to the unthrown rider.

Seeing them safely home, Sun Father smiled on high.

And thus was the horse given to The People.

II. The Sun Father's Horse

A CONTEMPORARY NAVAJO MYTH

Riding into the first light of the sun, Bluejay said the morning prayer of hozhoni.

> May all be well above me
> May all be well below me
> May all be well all around me
> The sky, be well
> The earth, be well
> The light, the darkness
> The mystery that is fire
> The prayer that is water
> In harmony it is done
> In harmony it is finished
> May harmony be all around me
> All the days of my life

Memory brought it back, the old trail of childhood up the foot of Rainy Butte. Tying his horse to a tree, he went up the butte on foot. The climb was much harder than he remembered. His legs were older, less sure of themselves. As he climbed he blessed his legs, his feet, his boots. And climbing, kept climbing.

What he found, he knew—the trail coming back into himself. This was how he started out, how his people started out; and it was how the Sun Father's son long ago started out. It was all-familiar to him, the jagged rocks, the slippery jointed cracks, the slick cobble, the falling-off places. At the top in the dawn sun, he prayed again.

> I walk in plain sight of my home
> I am at the entrance of my home
> I am in the middle of my home
> I am at the back of my home
> I am at the top of the pollen footprint
> Before me it is beautiful
> Behind me it is beautiful
> Under me it is beautiful
> Above me it is beautiful
> All around me it is beautiful

Bluejay felt himself rising and expanding with the words of the prayer. He felt the world echo with this simple expansion of himself. The brightness all around him turned brighter. And something happened. His father's medicine words came back to him: "Don't be afraid of what you see up there."

The horse came suddenly out of the sun—a golden horse with a mane of sun rays, with feet of flint butterflies that clattered on the clouds. It came out of the sun and thundered upon the clouds and kicked lightning loose on the world. Bluejay trembled at the sight of it, but he remembered what his father had said.

The horse came right at him, its nostrils flaring, an aura of pollen shining around its head, a song coming from its hooves, a dancing, wild-prancing golden horse with a wildflower hanging in a corner of its mouth.

It galloped at him. He closed his eyes, praying softly. The horse was almost on him. He could feel its oncoming surge, the force of its body moving through the light of morning. It will crush me, *he thought,* it will surely crush my bones to dust. *But his father's words returned to him again and again, until he was repeating them like a chant.*

Then he closed his eyes and the horse came on into the night of his head, a sunbeam in its mouth for a bridle. He wanted to dive under its terrible hooves, but he held to the vow of his father's words. Sucking his breath deep within the cave of his bones, he released his fear. He gave out a great shuddering of breath into the morning air. His shoulders fell; his head drooped.

And the horse of the sun passed lightly through him. He felt it enter him. Go through him. Go beyond him. He opened his eyes. The horse was going down the steep trail to the foot of Rainy Butte. He saw the golden white of its tail flick furiously as it danced down the rocky trail, a cloud of dust rising in its wake.

In the gentle rain that fell after the horse passed, Bluejay sang the song of the Sun Father's horse.

IV

EUROPE

16

The God Horse

SPANISH BARB

Three thousand years ago in the plains of Arabia and Barbary, there were swift, fine-mettled horses that were taken there by Phoenician ships, which were loaded down with iron, dye, and spice. But their most precious cargo was the Spanish Barb horse.

Descended from the North African Barb, this magnificent horse was also brought into Europe by the Berber horsemen of the eighth century. Although the bloodline was mixed with Arabian stock in Spain, the Barb's genetic traits remained dominant.

The Arabian and the Barb, however, made the Spanish horse—and this, as we know, was the cornerstone for all future American horse breeds. Moreover, without them, the English Thoroughbred would not be what it is today.

The Numidian horsemen of North Africa were among the first riders to demonstrate the Barb's grace and agility. These coastal warriors thundered into Carthage and helped to bring about its downfall. The Barb has been somewhat credited with the outcome of this great historic battle. (Interestingly, the Carthaginian mule came about because Barb mares drank from the same watering holes as the African wild asses. We wonder at the imagined beauty of a Barb mule!)

According to Barb breeder Olivia Tsosie, the Barb's history is neither etched in stone or in ink, but is yet to be accurately written:

> Recently I saw a show of fifteenth- and sixteenth-century drawings at the National Gallery in Washington, D.C. The horses those Germans drew were exactly the size and shape of Barbs. You can tell the size by checking how far the riders' feet come below the horse's barrel. They look amazingly like the Codex horses depicted by the Aztecs in their drawings of the Conquest. Incidentally, the newly restored paintings in the Palace of the Te show that Gonzaga horses were the most famous racing horses in sixteenth-century Europe—Tunisian Barbs. The route from Tunisia to Sicily was a short hop, another short hop to Naples and the mainland. A pair of Barbs was sent to Henry the VIII as presents.

History does state that Richard II's Barb, which was well known as Roan Barbary, was adored by the king, as he put it, like "an only son." Undeniably, this king was greatly attached to his horse—so much so that poets, dramatists, and writers of romance have immortalized Roan Barbary in their verses and tales.

Supposedly, King Richard's rage at hearing that Bolingbroke had chosen Roan Barbary upon which to ride to Westminster when he went there to be crowned was a standard theme for a great many authors, including, of course, William Shakespeare: "When Bolinbroke rode on Roan Barbary, that horse that thou so often hast bestrid" *(Richard II)*.

In fact, Henry Bolingbroke, John of Gaunt's son, deposed Richard II in 1399 and imprisoned him in Pontefract Castle, where the king later died, but not without having seen his hated rival ride to glory on his dear Barb horse.

The legendary Barb turns up again in the literature of the Godolphin—one of the foundation horses of the English Thoroughbred. This Barb came from the stables of the sultan of Morocco. In *King of the Wind*, Marguerite Henry reveals how the golden-coated foal, shortly after being born, nearly lost its life. Accordingly, when the horse boy presented the little foal, the chief groom spied a cross graining of hairs upon it that looked like a ripened beard of wheat.

> "The wheat ear!" Señor Achmet's voice broke. "It foretells evil. The droning of the bittern last night warned me. The yellow-eyed owl warned me. Ill luck will attend the colt's days. Ill luck will hang low over the royal stables."
>
> His eyes fixed on the foal's chest. He got slowly to his feet, drawing the saber at his belt. Agba smothered a cry. Unmindful of his own safety he thrust himself between Señor Achmet and the foal. He fell to his knees, lifting the tiny foal whose legs beat a tattoo in the air. With a look of triumph he pointed to the white spot on the off hind heel.
>
> Señor Achmet's eyes narrowed. His brows came together in a black line. Agba could see him weighing the two in his mind—

the white spot against the wheatear. The good sign against the bad. The scales tipped even.

Just at that moment the wild boar let out a squeal of anger. It reminded Señor Achmet that the boar's sole purpose in the royal stables was to turn away evil spirits from the horses and receive them into his own body. Grudgingly the groom sheathed his saber.

So goes the unproven but nonetheless plausible tale of the fine-blooded equine, which became a carthorse in Paris after Louis XV dismissed him as a gift on the bad advice of Bishop Fleury.

The six Moroccan gift horses were considered bony little broomtails when they were put beside the hefty warhorses of the king.

So the gift of Sultan Mulai Ismael unintentionally insulted the heavy-boned horse of France. This was made worse by the sultan's suggestion that his desert breed would strengthen and improve the king's own stock.

If the story is true as it has been retold over the centuries, the great Eastern horse had a long way to go before he was recognized as "King of the Wind" by the twinkling gray eyes of the earl of Godolphin, who saw in him an ancestry of greatness and the possibility of a fabulous future.

Marguerite Henry's premise is that there would have been no Man O'War, the greatest racer of his time, without "the fiery little horse from Morocco."

And yet all of this mythology hinges on a crinkly question mark. Was the Godolphin Arabian *really* a Barb?

Barb enthusiasts emphatically say yes.

Those who side with the Arabian take a "purer" point of view and say no.

The question is perhaps a nonquestion, since the blood of each Iberian horse is mixed—one part Barb, one part Arabian—and cannot be separated, per se.

In any event, we do know that there was Eastern equine blood throughout the Old World—Asia, Africa, Europe, and Asia Minor.

But the Iberian horse did not arrive in the New World until Columbus's arrival late in the fifteenth century.

On his first expedition, Columbus left thirty horses on the island of Hispaniola. Twenty years later, the population of horses in the West Indies had increased greatly, but when Cortez went to Mexico some one hundred years after, he virtually rode into his own legend.

When the Aztecs saw their first horseman, they viewed man and horse as one, considering the fusion to be a singular creature of magic. The Plains Indians, too, bowed before the horse, seeing in it the beauty of no other earthly animal—it therefore had to be a god.

To the Dakota, it was *sunka wakan*, or mystery dog.

To the Shawnee, *mishawa*, or elk, a spirit animal.

To the tribes of North America in general, the horse became a companion on the hunt and bearer of burdens, but more than this, the four-footed mystery beast was a great friend.

No doubt, the horse mobilized the American Indian and created a new economy based upon a "horse standard of wealth." As a medium of exchange the horse became, in addition, an incentive for tribal warfare. Foot-wandering, farming tribes like the Sioux, once they were mounted, lived a different life, a warlike one that was horse dependent and horse solvent. This would not change until the end of the nineteenth century.

And to think that all of this began with the coming of Cortez. Fortunately, the literature of the horse in the Americas begins with an ironclad description from Bernard Diaz del Castillo, Cortez's historian, who accurately itemizes the equines on board ship in 1519.

A light chestnut stallion which presently died.
An excellent chestnut mare for sport and for racing.
A silver gray mare of good racing quality.
Another silver gray mare, a good racer, very powerful and restless.
A light chestnut stallion, with three white feet; no good.
A silver gray mare, barren. Fair but a poor racer.
A perfect chestnut, which ran very well.

A dun stallion with black points, does not go well.

A very good stallion, light chestnut and a good racer.

An excellent dark stallion, called Muleteer; one of the good
horses we brought in the fleet.

A chestnut mare. This foaled on the ship.

The favorite mount—and the most famous legendary horse in the
New World—was Cortez's own mount, Morzillo, a black Spanish
Barb stallion. The name means "black with a reddish luster."

Morzillo, though short-lived in the flesh, grew immortal in spirit.
It happened on the way to Honduras. Morzillo got a large splinter
in his hoof. Two rafts ferried him across the river—one for his front
end and one for his rear.

However, the poor horse suffered from bad water, poor rations,
and vampire bats that fed on him each night. When the splinter sunk
deep, the horse's fate was sealed.

Not knowing what else to do, Cortez left his once lovely Barb with
the Indians in the village of Lake Peten. He gave instructions on
Morzillo's care and feeding, and he told the Indians that he would
return for his horse, and they had better take good care of him.

From here on, the history is hazy, but we suspect the Aztecs took
Cortez's threat seriously. They treated El Morzillo like a god. They
kept him in a temple, and they fed him chicken, coconut meat,
pomegranates, papayas, figs, bananas, and various tropical flowers.
Of course, the great horse could not survive on this food and eventually starved to death.

The second-century Roman emperor Verus fed his Arabian horse
a diet of raisins and almonds, and reportedly the horse lived. But not
Morzillo. After his death, the Aztecs kept him alive, spiritually, by
carving a stone statue of Morzillo sitting on his haunches. They
called their effigy *Tziminchac*, god of thunder and lightning.

From then on, Morzillo, the Spanish Barb, was a deity.

One hundred years later, two Spanish missionaries arrived in
Honduras, and when they saw the statue of the horse, they demol-
ished it. Yet they could not destroy the spiritual presence of Morzillo

because the great horse was now a part of the earth and sky, and even today his shadow is seen rippling on the bottom of Lake Peten.

That is the story, but like all interesting and lasting horse myths, there is more to it than that. For one thing, the equine image of a seated horse is a real puzzlement.

Cunninghame Graham *(The Horses of the Conquest)* explains why he thinks El Morzillo was sitting on his haunches:

> They placed before him food . . . almonds and raisins with which Lucius Verres fed his horse. Maidens all garlanded with flowers tempted the victim with fruits and chickens and all the chiefest delicacies they could find. Their efforts were in vain, and the poor horse, a reasonable animal enough in his own fashion, eventually died. One hundred seventy two years later, another expedition, with its usual accompaniment of padres, came through that wilderness, and in poking around an island in a great river of many channels, found one of the strangest, and yet in its implications, one of the most thrilling deities raised by the hands of wild but worshipful men. It was the stone figure of a horse sitting upon its hunkers; a monument to El Morzillo, the black horse that had come as companion to the leader of their conquerors.

Graham believed the stone effigy shows an oddly disfigured, seated horse. Naturally, horses do not, unless under special circumstances, assume this position, and Graham's supposition is this: "In the somber reflection induced by death, men are inclined to recall the last impression of the revered objects of their affections. They may have fashioned El Morzillo's likeness in the last vivid image that fastened itself unforgettably upon their memories. Thus one of the horses of the conquest became immortal and a god."

During the Middle Ages in Europe, horses were primarily utilitarian animals. They were not considered magical or sacred, yet as war machinery they were quite expendable. In fact, many a warhorse died violently, as is richly and wretchedly attested in the chronicles of King Arthur. Knights usually had spares, as it were, close at hand, and the idea of the horse as a commodity, or something with replacement value (as an automobile is today) might very well stem from its use, or misuse, on European battlefronts.

In *The Second Tale of Sir Lancelot*, a bedraggled horse comes out of the forest

> riderless, with broken reins, a shattered saddlebow and stirrup leathers all stained with blood. Then they feared the worst. Gawain was some way ahead of the rest and shortly he saw coming towards him a knight, whose horse was panting hoarsely and lathered in sweat. Recognizing Gawain, the knight stopped and said, "My lord Gawain, as you can see my horse is at the end of his strength and I cannot ride him further. I pray you lend or give me one of your two spare horses; I promise to pay you back later."

Horse skulls and equine bones *have always embodied magical or sacred properties.* The skulls of horses were once set upon the gables of houses to offer protection and bring good fortune. Horse bones were used in prophecy and healing rituals, too.

Once in northern New Mexico we found the bleached bones of a horse scattered in an arroyo for over six miles. A flash flood had taken the poor animal by surprise. Drowned, the flesh desiccated and the bones disassembled, and what was left of the horse was polished by the sun and the desert air. You could count the bones, each a sand-polished gemstone, piled in one place and then another, for miles.

The beautifully flute-shaped neck, swanlike and firm, pretty in its bed of mica schist, stood out strangely against the ochre sand. Once, we knew, this horse had stood proud—mane to the wind, moon in the eye—drinking the wind. But now it was scattered on the same track it had walked, trotted, cantered, and galloped.

There was something holy about the bright-toothed head, so we brought it home, put it in a window alcove—why, we couldn't have said exactly, but it was somehow lovely and of the desert, and it felt safer having it there in the window casement with the mouth biting the sun and moon and stars, a fitting tribute, we thought, to the greatness of the animal it had been and should always remain.

The Characteristics of the Spanish Barb

This unique horse came close to being absorbed into the general horse population until a small-scale breeding program was carried on by some families and ranchers and the Spanish Barb Breeders Association, started in 1972.

The Spanish Barb might reflect either Barb or Iberian heritage. If Barb, he will have a narrower chest and slightly angular croup. If Iberian, he will have a rounder croup and broader chest. Either way, the Spanish Barb should have an overall image of balance. He stands fourteen to fifteen hands.

The profile is straight to slightly convex, with short ears that are often notched. The back is short to medium with strong haunches. The mane and tail should be full. The Spanish Barb appears in a wide variety of colors and shades: black, sorrel, chestnut, roan, grullo, dun, and buckskin. His strength of spirit and vitality add to his great physical attributes to make him an excellent horse for trail riding, endurance riding, and ranch work.

17

The Gypsy Horse of the Sea

CAMARGUE

The coastal area in the south of France that embraces the Ile de Camargue lies in summer under a scorching sun, but when winter comes the land is bitten by the cold Alpine winds. Not an ideal location for a horse—unless it's the coarse-faced, short-necked, big-hoofed Camargue, which is born black or brown and turns white-gray as it gets older.

The Camargue has an enduring mythology, as fantastic as it is memorable and even biblical. Historically, the horse resembles the cave drawings at Lascaux and Niaux that go back to 15,000 B.C.

The Camargue has been living in the triangular-shaped Rhone Delta, a mixed landscape of scrub plains and salt marsh, since ancient times. Here, the mistral blows and softly sheets the ground with cold salt water and brings with it the unpleasant weather the Camargue horse seems to thrive on.

Through the centuries, many armies—Greeks, Romans, Arabs, Gypsies—marched through here on their way to somewhere else, and their definitive horse breeds influenced the blood of the Camargue. Today the Gypsies still pay homage to the horse of their ancestors. How this came to be is very interesting.

Above the tile roofs of the town of Saintes-Maries-de-la-Mer, the Rom gather each year to honor the myth of Sarah, the servant girl who is their patron saint. How sainthood got bridled to the Camargue horse is shrouded in mystery, but residents say that in A.D. 42 two sisters of the Virgin Mary landed on the shore of this town.

According to the myth, the female voyagers became known as regionally recognized saints: Saint Mary Jacobe and Saint Mary Salome.

How did they get there, and why are they so important to the Gypsy community?

Again, legend tells us that they drifted to southern France in their small open boat, a craft that had neither oars nor sails. Coming all the way from the Holy Land, they had with them only their servant girl, Sarah, to whom the Rom pay homage each year on the twenty-fourth and the twenty-fifth of May. Although this is said to be the oldest pilgrimage in France, the Gypsies didn't associate with it until the nineteenth century.

Sarah, the Marys' servant girl, is neither a saint of the church nor a proven historical figure. Instead she exists solely in the annals of folklore. Nonetheless, Sarah draws forth thousands of Gypsies, who pay their respects with lighted candles, songs, processions, and celebrations of all kinds.

The main procession to the sea is like a parade syncopated by clomping Camargue hooves that ring on the cobblestones of Saintes-Maries-de-la-Mer.

Riding the rugged Camargue horses are *gardians*—the riders known as Camargue cowboys. So, down to the sea they clatter on their rugged, snow-white cow ponies. And as the statues of the two Marys are borne aloft through the town, the horses keep time with them, clipping and clopping, until the procession reaches the blue-green Mediterranean Sea, and the statues are dipped three times, thus returning to the sea that which was given to the shore some two thousand years earlier.

To Gypsy culture worldwide, the Camargue is a focal point of this celebration, as this particular horse—as well as horses in general—have always been a big part of Romany lives and livelihood. Yes, long has the horse been revered by the Rom. The reason is self-evident, for they have ever been a people on the move, and the equine was necessary to them—for travel and trade and as a bridge between the Rom and the *gażo*, or the culture at large.

On horse and in wagon, the Gypsy really achieved a mobile, if greatly dispersed, international identity. Traditionally the horse was the thing that linked them to the outside world. However, the Gypsies were much more than horse traders—they were the original *whisperers*. Indeed, they were also tradesmen, tinkers, and blacksmiths, and the secrets of their horse lore date back thousands of years.

The Gypsy horse arts, so to say, made an indelible contribution to the societies around them, and allowed them to enter the workaday world without a fixed abode.

Gypsy horse traders were unique, for they raised horses as family members, bringing them up in the world as Rom—which meant teaching them to understand Romany rather than any other language. In addition, the Gypsy's gentleness with equine training was really unknown in many European countries.

Since such a horse was so raised, it would not, customarily, answer to *gaźo* commands; as a result, it was often returned to the Romany owner. Legend holds that the Gypsy horse trader gave back only *half* of the purchase price of the horse, however. Naturally he maintained that there was nothing really wrong with the animal's sensitivity to command. And when he spoke to it in his own language, the horse acted accordingly, much to the amazement of the confused *gaźo* buyer.

There are many similar stories in Gypsy horse culture. According to Michael Stewart *(The Time of the Gypsies)*, a mare in the Gypsy stable, if returned, bought, or traded back, was always given a special feminine welcoming by the boys of the family. Her mane was plaited all the way down one side of her neck. Also, on the way to a Gypsy wedding, a white mare displayed white scarves belonging to her owner's wife. At the wedding ceremony itself, the wife was expected to retrieve these scarves and wear them on her own head. Thus did woman and horse change identity.

Moreover, just as a woman's hair was considered sacred (an emblem of her fertility), so was the horse's tail. In general, the likeness of Romany women to Romany horses was expressed in many poetical, allegorical, and purely economical ways, and there is a Czech Gypsy saying, a libation with wine, that goes "To the beauty of our horses and the strength of our women."

Horse metaphors—those dealing with money and child-rearing—occur frequently in Gypsy dialogue today, as they did hundreds of years ago, and there is always a sense of the mystery of equine and feminine behavior and a feeling of adoration for each.

In the culture at large, this same mystery is frequently abusive rather than affectionate, but in Gypsy culture, especially long ago, the horse-woman comparison had much in common with the old earth religions of ancient India, and it was not derided or misused.

The story is told, however, of the Gypsy man who is soon to marry the woman of his choice. The bride-to-be, just before reaching the altar, is upstaged by a clever mare, so it is the horse that gets the man instead of the woman.

The story is also told of the man who wishes to buy a horse, which the owner will not sell. The mare, says the owner, is the most valuable thing he owns. In time, though, the horse-seeking man discovers the owner has a beautiful daughter, and, in romantic Gypsy fashion, he runs away with her astride the sought-after horse.

The owner, having lost his precious daughter and his finest horse, decides in the end that he might as well accept the thief because, for one thing, the man has impeccable taste in women and a great mastery of the horse. He concludes without a hint of rancor, "My daughter and my horse are safe with this man, and the marriage will indeed prove worthy on account of this."

In contemporary times, Gypsy culture seems to have lost its affinity with horses. Much of that old, lovely equine grace is gone or in sad decline, except perhaps in the use of the Romany language.

Gone, too, is the special, mystic relationship between horses and women—and, for that matter, between women and men.

Isabel Fonseca (Bury Me Standing: The Gypsies and Their Journey) tells the true story of traveling with a modern Romany family, who, from the safety of their car, witness the removal of a dead horse along the side of an Albanian road.

The animal is winched and dragged into a waiting cart and is hauled off so unceremoniously, so degradingly, that she poignantly writes, "In the days that followed, the horse was never mentioned. In a protective gesture of unspoken but unmistakable admonition, Jeta silenced my inquiry—not, I inferred, because the animal had died gruesomely, but because of residual respect for an honored beast."

And it is that very thing, that residual respect for a mythically honored animal, that we recognize in the faces of the penitents, who chant the praises of Saint Sarah and bow their heads lovingly to the Camargue.

The life of the Camargue's owner, the Gypsy trader, was never easy, and often it was extremely hard. A horse dealer had to be many other things if he wanted to stay alive. His many occupations included farrier, knife grinder, fortune-teller, chicken plucker, and piano tuner—virtually anything that would make money quickly and enable the practitioner to get from town to town.

Nor was caring for a horse on the road an easy thing. The Gypsy was often hard-pressed to get good hay. He had to beg and borrow, and as one Gypsy writer put it, "There are not so many hairs on my head as the number of times I have begged bread on the streets of a village."

In summer, life was good, but in winter it was always a trial, and Gypsy mothers would sooner take the blankets off their children and put them on their shivering horses than let their animals suffer.

On summer evenings, however, there were familial horse groomings. On such occasions, villagers stole away from their farms to be with the Gypsies, just to learn what they knew about horses. Townsfolk liked safe swapping and noncompetitive trading, and they liked hearing about life on the road and under the open sky. Social visits like these weren't risky, and they usually ended well. Some didn't, though. We read of one gathering that ended in a terrible battle between "townies" and Gypsies, with iron spoons and pitchforks being brandished and a number of people on both sides getting hurt over a needless misunderstanding.

Road life of the true Gypsy vanished more than four decades ago, but memories of Romany horse lore still haunt the writings of international horse trainer Linda Tellington-Jones, who recounts the old Gypsy tradition of "horse-face personality analysis."

This is a system that uses the placement and number of swirls on a horse's head as a guide to character and temperament.

She learned this, she says, from her grandfather Will Caywood, who worked as a trainer for Czar Nicholas II. He got it from the Russian Gypsy who was his translator. Tellington-Jones describes this in *Getting in TTouch: Understand and Influence Your Horse's Personality.* "The art of personality analysis is an ancient one, traditional in a number of cultures that held horses in high regard as individual beings. Interestingly, the Gypsies of Europe and Asia, renowned for centuries for their special relationship with horses, used a method of personality analysis also employed by those great equine experts of North African and Arabian deserts, the Bedouins."

Facial swirls are the equine equivalent of human fingerprints. The swirl's shape and precise location on the horse's face reveal hidden aspects of the animal's personality.

A swirl, or whorl, as it is sometimes called, is a distinctive pattern of hair. If you see a single one between or above the eyes, the horse could have an uncomplicated personality. A swirl several inches below the eyes often indicates an imaginative and intelligent horse; these equines, says Tellington-Jones, are the ones that turn on water faucets and open stall doors.

Tellington-Jones has had years of experience in evaluating swirls. She confirms that they do, in fact, give away definite characteristics in the horses that she has studied and whose lives she has followed up on.

Once, while visiting a ranch in Israel, she found an intractable horse whose owner was at the point of putting him down. The animal kicked and bit and was difficult to saddle and mount. "He had to be cross-tied, and it took two people on either side to lead him."

However, when she saw that this horse "had a long swirl on the forehead extending several inches below the eyes," she was surprised because this generally revealed a horse with a friendly personality. So she felt there must be another cause for the disturbance. Sure enough, she found it in sore spots on the horse's neck and withers.

The fit of the saddle, she discovered, "was one of the worst I have ever encountered. The pommel sat directly on his withers, and the gullet pressed directly on points below and behind the withers. Pressure on these points caused pain and also affected the horse's diaphragm, interfering with his breathing."

After doing her "TTouch" massage on the painful areas, Tellington-Jones was able to relieve the horse's misery to the degree that his owner—after the treatment was complete—could not believe he was the same horse. So the swirl gave evidence not of a *difficult* horse but an *afflicted* one.

The Characteristics of the Camargue

The Camargue horse is born black or brown and turns whitish-gray as it gets older. It stands between thirteen and fourteen hands and has a large, square head with wide-set, expressive eyes and short, broad-based ears. The neck is deep at the base and quite muscular. The chest is wide and deep, the croup short and narrow. The shoulder is straight and short, and the mane and tail are long and thick.

This is an even-tempered, active horse that is particularly good at going long distances, enduring rough weather, existing on little food, and being an all-round hardy riding horse.

The breed is strictly protected by the Biological Research Station Latour du Valat in the Camargue. The Camargue Regional Park was established in 1928 to save the indigenous horses and cattle from human encroachment. In the isolated environment provided, people have been permitted to watch the life, manners, and breeding of this essentially wild horse. The Camargue has, in this way, contributed greatly to our understanding of uninfluenced equine behavior.

18

The High–Stepping Stallion

LIPIZZAN

Four hundred years of exceptional breeding have made the high-stepping stallion what it is today, yet long ago the horse was neither grand nor glorious and hardly a high-stepper. She was a horse of the mountains, the Karst horse. The Karst was a small primal equine named after the Slovenian wilderness whence it came. This was, indeed, a rough and rocky land, and it gave birth to a rough-edged, rock-hard little horse.

The true breed of the Lipizzan began in 1880 with Archduke Charles II. He got Andalusians, Berbers, and Barbs from the Iberian Peninsula and bred them with the Karst horse. In time a purebred horse emerged from this union—a great white equine that became indelibly attached to the city of Vienna.

The attachment came about because Charles II also created a Spanish Riding School as an adjunct to the Hapsburg court. The object was to provide the nobility with a complete education in the equestrian arts. The result was, and is, the oldest riding academy in the world. And, some say, the finest horse to go with it.

Today the magnificence of the Lipizzan is quite equal with the Viennese Riding Hall, which is a miracle all by itself. It resembles a drawing or reception room perhaps more than it does an exercise ring. How that happened is yet another story, but one worth repeating here.

Austrian architect Fischer von Erlach was also a dreamer. In 1729 he borrowed the plans drawn up by Mansart for the chapel at Versailles. These were what he used to build the grand hall—fifty-five meters long by eighteen meters wide surrounded by forty-six Corinthian columns that support the upper gallery.

The only color in the pristine white hall is the raked red sawdust down below and the scarlet velvet gallery railings up above. Add to this the dazzle of the heavily made, mythically shaped, arch-necked, trotting white stallions, and you understand why seeing them, as if bursting with sunlight, is a revered and unmatched equine spectacle.

When Lipizzans move, the heart goes with them. When they perform what is called "the passage," they seem to spring upward, barely skimming the ground, their great weight changed into volatile vapor. The miracle of the Lipizzan's leap is that this light-footed grace is so natural as to seem inevitable, an act of nature rather than an inbred skill that defies nature. Well, perhaps it is both.

Amazingly, even colts of this breed enjoy this gravity-defying grace. The U.S. Lipizzan Horse Registry says, "Even difficult dressage such as 'the airs above the ground'—*levade, courbette, ballotade*—can be witnessed from the time a colt is only a few days old and they are easily elicited later."

Lipizzans have been called the most easily trainable horses in the entire equine kingdom. Their attention span and memory are remarkable, and they can be taught multiple moves without any loss of patience or concentration.

Perhaps these are just some of the things that caught the eye of General George S. Patton at the close of World War II, when he witnessed what might very well have been the demise of this great breed.

While bombs were falling on Vienna in 1945, Patton, the conquering hero, saw the Lipizzans in a private performance that amazed, distressed, and puzzled him. He was not, as some would say, totally won over by the magnificence of the horsemanship or the purity of the breed, yet he would devote himself to resurrecting both of these nobilities rather single-handedly.

Actually, Patton saw the horses and their riders as superfluous beauty—this in juxtaposition to the war effort, which was not yet over. As he put it,

> It struck me as rather strange that, in the midst of a world at war, some twenty young and middle-aged men in great physical condition, together with about thirty grooms, had spent their entire time teaching a group of horses to wriggle their butts and raise their feet in consonance with certain signals from the heels and reins. Much as I like horses, this seemed to me wasted energy. On the other hand, it is probably wrong to permit any highly developed art, no matter how fatuous, to perish from the earth—and which arts are fatuous depends on the point of view.

To me the high schooling of horses is certainly more interesting
than either painting or music.

Vienna in the spring of 1945 was under siege and being bom-
barded. The renowned Spanish Riding School was under the direction of Colonel Alois Podhajsky, who had ingeniously smuggled all
of the Lipizzans in the school to a small village in lower Austria, near
Linz, where he hoped they would be safe from the advancing
Russian army.

Yet, as food for the horses became scarce, so did sustenance for
the nearby Red Army. Podhajsky then begged help from the
American officers with whom he was in contact—and, fortunately,
it was Patton himself who took charge. After having witnessed the
Lipizzans in winged motion, Patton sat moodily, stonily. He seemed,
in fact, to be unmoved. Podhajsky rode up to him with a sweepingly
courteous gesture of his hat.

"We ask your protection," he said.

Patton, poker-faced, nodded.

Then he said in a gravelly voice, "Magnificent!"

After which he gave his promise that the Lipizzans would be
wards of the U.S. Army until they could be returned to the "new
Austria." Had General Patton not done this, the best scenario is that
the horses would have performed in Moscow for the Russian military elite. The worst probability is that the close-quartered, half-
starved Russian Army could have devoured them.

Patton has been praised for his seemingly unselfish act of equine
devotion, but he was a complex and perverse man who often acted
on passion and whim. In any case, his word on these horses became
law. They survived the war, and we have Patton and Podhajsky to
thank for it.

In mythology, the big, white, cloud-footed stallion is Pegasus. Sired
by the sea god, Poseidon, and mothered by the gorgon, Medusa, this
horse was the quintessence of all that is equine—powerful, graceful,
and infinitely wise.

How he came to be born is magical and alchemical.

When the droplets of blood from the Medusa's severed head spattered the sea foam, Poseidon made them into the winged steed known as Pegasus. Snowy white and strong, Pegasus became the first member of the equine race to ever bear a human rider on his back.

In time, Apollo and the Muses rode about on Pegasus. But it wasn't until the coming of Bellerophon that a mortal really sat astride him for the first time. His legendary use of this horse is also very magical.

Under the altar of Athene, Bellerophon fell asleep and dreamed. In his dream, Athene gave him a golden bridle. Awakening, he saw that it was so—the brilliant bridle lay at his side. With this, he was able to tame the elusively shy Pegasus. When the horse's sun-cloven hooves touched the earth and he drank at the spring of Pirene, Bellerophon caught hold of him and bridled him.

Soon thereafter, Bellerophon was assigned the terrible task of killing the Chimera—the *mingled-monster*, Homer called it.

Without the immortal horse of Olympus he might not have succeeded, for the Chimera was a flaming fusion of lion, goat, and serpent that had a very bad temper. Yet Pegasus put the hero over the top, and the Chimera was slain.

Bellerophon took many flights on Pegasus's back, but in the end he got himself in trouble by hanging out at Olympus. A mere mortal was not supposed to ascend to such heights, even if he did ride a celestial steed. So Jupiter sent a gadfly to bite Pegasus. When the great horse bolted, Bellerophon fell to earth. Blinded from his fall, he was never to ride Pegasus again.

The Hippocrene, or Horse's Fountain, was on Mount Helicon in Boeotia. Its sacred waters were known to confer poetic inspiration to all who drank from them. Keats longed for a drink from this sacred fountain—"a beaker of the full warm south."

Longfellow called the horse waters "Maddening draughts of Hippocrene."

In fact, the word *hippocrene* comes from *hippeia*, or "of the horse."

Speaking of water and horses, Poseidon, god of the sea, was a great horse lover. By siring a "horse child" with Athene, who was a goddess of the earth, he joined the worlds, making them one. Between the two was the immortal, winged horse—and this magic still exists in our collective unconscious today.

One more Poseidon legend, a lesser-known one, is that he wooed the goddess Ceres, who changed herself into a horse. The only way Poseidon could catch her was to make himself into an equine, too. Thus did he become the sire of Arion, the winged horse that had the power of speech. This ancient myth has been with humans since the first horse was sought and seen, and it accounts for our persistent love of talking horses.

So, with the Lipizzan what we see *is* what we get, a horse the equal of our favorite horse myth—Pegasus. Moreover, the Lipizzan is foam white and as light as air. And when he leaves the ground, he transcends gravity and—truly seeming to fly—becomes the living legend of the Greeks and Romans.

In appearance, he resembles Pegasus, too. His aura is so sunny that when turned out, or ridden, his head rises, his neck arches, and he looks quite emblematic—Pegasus come to life, soaring toward the sun.

In manner, once again, the Lipizzan has the gentle nobility of the horse of myth, for if you approach him with a kindly word, he is docile and humble, and yet a prouder equine was never bridled by gold, dream, or mortal rider. The Lipizzan, it is said, does not grow old but stays steady under saddle, elegant to the end.

The Lipizzan is one of the only equines who, physically and spiritually, is transformational by nature. That is to say, for the first three years of his life, this horse is dark or bay colored. After the third year, he begins to turn white, turning fully so in his seventh year. Consider, then, the symbolism of three and its particular relationship to this horse.

The number three is blessed.

There are the three ages of our lives—childhood, youth, and adulthood.

There are the three times of day—morning, noon, and night.

And there is always the lucky number three, as in fairy tales that offer the questing hero or heroine three magic wishes.

Seven is, of course, another magic number, as in the seven deadly sins, so called. And their opposite, the alleged seven years of fulfillment. This was the time necessary for culmination or fruition in the medieval cycle of life.

These mystical numbers figure prominently in the psychic world—and so, as we have been saying, does the horse.

Color, too, is a psychic value paid tribute by our ancient ancestors. White, the color of the Lipizzan, was considered long ago to be the hue of purity, the color of the morning sun.

As such, the Lipizzan figured prominently in dreams and myths of purification and cleansing. Trained to leap beyond its earthly orbit, the Lipizzan goes through an alchemical change of a kind. It overleaps dross matter, gross weight, and gravity and achieves a kind of longevity.

The grace of horses in general has much to do with the mortal belief that beauty can overcome ugliness and cancel out death. So many of our fairy tales aim at achieving a harmonic resolution and, quite often, horses are the means to this end.

There is the prince's white horse at the awakening of Snow White from her deep, still sleep. And in the Russian folktale "The Little Magic Horse," the deformed hero, a hunchback, performs great deeds in the service of her owner. At the end of the story, after a milk bath, she turns into a glimmering, sunlit mare.

The white horse in mythology is life, death, and the hereafter all rolled into one. Moreover, as the Lipizzan really changes physically during its first three years of life and begins to turn white only after that time, it is a transformational animal, an archetypal changing horse, one that starts out plain and mundane and after three years grows into another order of being. This caused metaphysicians from the Middle Ages to imagine that the horse was alchemical. The turning of prime matter into quicksilver is the very core of medieval alchemy. Animals, in nature, might, through a natural process, change mysteriously and gloriously—so why couldn't people? Or could they? The first book of animal changes was *The Bestiary* of the Middle Ages, and it did a pretty good job of classifying beasts, both magical and mundane, throughout the world.

Nine hundred years later, Carl Jung, in trying to come to grips with the human psyche, saw "the changes" that humans go through as the male principle of consciousness uniting with the female. The unconscious, too, included a bestiary of strange creatures, not unlike and often including the ones in the early Christian bestiaries. It seems, as humans, we never outgrew our childlike fear and fantasy of being part-human and part-horse, or part-man and part-woman.

Well, perhaps this *is* a lot to lay at the hooves of an innocent equine, but if we look at the Lipizzan's legendary, emblematic history as well as its physical incarnation from a dark and gangly colt to a full-bodied snowy horse, we may see why our ancestors paid such homage to an animal that expressed their innermost belief in mutability, in the magic cycle of change and transformation.

The Lipizzan is a kind of leap of faith all by herself. Wingless, she soars as if winged. Our hearts soar when we see her. In a performance of the dancing Lipizzan, we see ourselves lightened, brightened, and beautified—if only for a brief, incandescent second.

It's no wonder devout knights sought the Grail astride great white horses—horses the color *of whipped cream, sea foam, sea spume, white-lit fire.* In the Hindu Upanishads, white isn't just a symbol of psychic change but the alpha and omega of all change.

The Characteristics of the Lipizzan

Some people are surprised to learn that Lipizzans are not huge horses—seldom taller than sixteen hands. Because of their powerful movements and elastic muscular bodies, they appear much larger than they are. They do not mature until they are around seven, and their coats turn slowly from black or bay to a magnificent white by the time they are fully mature.

Another interesting maturation fact is that from about eight months to three years they go through an ugly-duckling stage when they don't even resemble the breed that they will later become. In Austria the young horses are taken to the Alps, where no tourists will view them, until they come out of this stage and into their final, mature form.

A Lipizzan, standing, looks heavy and lethargic, but as soon as he is mounted there is a rippling display of fiery emotion. However, this horse, as we've pointed out, is docile with people and adaptable to diverse situations. Perhaps this is the reason this unusual equine survived the many years of hiding and traveling around different parts of Europe during the world wars.

19

The Horse of the Tolt

ICELANDIC HORSE

I celand celebrates the classic beauty of the Icelandic horse in its national literature of ancient oral tales, *Njal's Saga*. Therein, the icecaps and dark igneous cliffs merge with gossamer waterfalls and icy glacial rivers and the small, thin-legged, full-maned horse that carried the ancient ones from rock to rill without injury to head or heart.

In Iceland today, off-road vehicles get stuck, overturn, and remain dependable only when they are fed gasoline. Not so the ever-practical horse. It is that kind of land, and the horse is more important in it than the Jeep.

After eleven centuries, the Icelandic horse still gets people across fast water; it is, they say, an inbred maneuver. Amazingly, she swims slightly cocked to one side, legs pointing downstream, which allows the rider, floating just upstream, to hold on to her mane while she swims across.

The first immigrants to Iceland came on open boats from Norway and from the Norse colonies of western Scotland, the Isle of Man, and Ireland. They brought horses with them from all of these regions—ponies of the British Isles and the Norwegian fjord from Norway—and these animals were indispensable to the settlers.

The Icelandic horse was not bred as a beast of burden. From the start, he was a riding horse and, in the eighth century, a real necessity for traveling anywhere in this rugged land. Rarely skittish, always gentle, the Icelandic horse's running walk is so smooth that a man's head does not bob when riding; and this must have been a great pleasure in a country of bumps and grinds and lots of uphill grades.

They say no other horse in the world has the fifth-geared gait of the Icelandic horse, and his other fine quality is an unerring sense of place. Horses sold in one part of the country can usually find their way back to their home farm, if they desire to do so.

According to David Roberts and Jon Krakauer *(Iceland: Land of the Sagas)*, "The Icelandic horse has an even purer pedigree than the Icelander himself. For more than eight hundred years, no horses have been imported into the country. A horse may be sold abroad, but once it has left Iceland, it can never return."

For all their love of these equines, however, the first settlers made horse stealing a capital crime, but they stopped short of forbidding the eating of horseflesh; this is not universally true, yet it is regionally true in certain parts of Iceland. Today, some herds are bred solely for their meat, while in other parts of Iceland, a man who accidentally eats horsemeat will expiate his crime by purging himself of it days and even weeks afterward.

The mythic sagas of Iceland incorporate the equine to a greater extent than almost any other nation. In *Hrafnkel's Saga*, for example, the hero adores his pale dun stallion with the black mane and black stripe down his back, whose name is Freyfaxi, as if he were a soul mate.

Indeed, Hrafnkel vows to kill anyone who rides his steed without permission. When his shepherd sneaks a ride on Freyfaxi, Hrafnkel finds out just by observing the behavior of his beloved horse: "Freyfaxi was all running with sweat; and every hair on his body was dripping. He was covered in mud and panting in exhaustion. He rolled over a dozen times, and then neighed loudly and started to race down the path."

In keeping with his vow, Hrafnkel slays the unfaithful shepherd as just retribution for disobedience. Morally, it seems, the Old Icelandic culture equated riding a man's horse without his consent to sleeping with his wife.

The earliest Icelandic bards sang the praises of their horses, as if they were, indeed, godlike beings. *Kelpie* legends flourished here as well as in the British Isles, and all in all the horse had a hold on these people that is nearly unmatched anywhere else except in the American Indian plains culture.

The oldest Norse oral narratives tell of a sacred tree that is the spiritual, or symbolic, spinal column of the cosmos. This tree was known as *Yggdrasil*. Perennially green, Yggdrasil was an ash whose roots pierced the subterranean kingdom as its branches and leaves were raised on high to the starlit heavens.

The legend of Yggdrasil is that Odin's charger, Sleipnir (which means "slipper"), browses among its boughs, making both the horse and the tree hallowed for all time.

They say that Odin's equine was gray, very much like the Icelandic clouds. Moreover, he trod on eight feet and was swifter than the wind when he galloped over the sea. There is a riddle about Sleipnir that goes . . .

Who are the two who ride to the Thing?
Three eyes they have together,
Ten feet and one tail.
And thus they travel through the lands.

The reason that Odin and his horse had but three eyes between them was that Odin voluntarily sacrificed one of his eyes so he could obtain Wisdom, the hallmark of his heroism.

Magic is also afoot in Odin's runic alphabet, which, according to myth, he invented himself, inscribing it on Sleipnir's teeth.

In one of the legends, the gods of Asgard are met by a mysterious stranger. The stranger offers to rebuild the wall that has just been destroyed in the war of the Aesir and the Vanir, two opposing factions.

Anyway, the gods of Asgard decide to take the stranger up on his offer. They feel quite defenseless against the frost giants, who, at any time, can stride into their kingdom.

So the stranger says he will rebuild the wall, but in return for this favor, he would like several things. He asks for the goddess Freya, the sun, and the moon.

The gods grumble at this, for it's a tall order, but they do not really fret because they cannot imagine that a man, a mere mortal, can accomplish so large a thing as the building of a world-sealing wall. He will try and fail, they agree. Still, they ask him a question.

"How will you build this mighty wall?"

"I will use my hands and my stallion."

At this, they all laugh.

However, in just a few days, the wall is almost done—and it is splendid, a fortification of great magnitude.

"How can a mortal perform such an immense task?" the gods of Asgard ask themselves. Finally they decide that the stranger must be a god, too, and his horse, a magic being.

Furthermore, they feel that the trickster Loki must have a hand in this mischievous deed. They are beside themselves, for now they must part with the goddess Freya as well as the sun and the moon.

Desperate to save face, Loki promises them he will find a way to trick the stranger and get the goddess and the sacred orbs back.

So that night a beautiful mare appears in the moonlight and draws the stranger's stallion off into the hills. No more stones are set in place, the great wall remains unfinished, and the goddess and the orbs are returned.

Now it happens that the great god Thor, who was away while this was happening, suddenly returns. He and the mysterious stranger quickly come to blows. They have an epic battle and, in the end, the stranger loses his life.

Months after, Loki gives birth to a gray colt, which has eight legs and looks exactly like the stranger's stallion. So, Odin, the great hero of the North, takes this equine for his own, and it becomes the legendary Sleipnir, the most powerful, magical horse of the nine worlds.

There seems to be an American presidential footnote, or *hoofnote*, with regard to the Icelandic horse. When Theodore Roosevelt was in office and his son Archibald was bedridden, the boy's brother took his horse, Algonquin, a calico Icelandic pony, up to the second floor of the White House, where, according to rumor, he helped the boy to recover.

The Characteristics of the Icelandic Horse

The Icelandic horse is small, the average height being thirteen to fourteen hands, and very sturdily built. Some say she is lacking in elegance, but the strongest characteristics are her versatility in performance riding, her workable character, and her lively temperament.

Though all colors are possible, the most common is chestnut. All white markings are acceptable to the breed standard, and pinto is very common. The mane and tail are long and luxurious, with the winter coat being double (the longer outer hairs covering a thick undercoat).

Although traditionally the Icelandic horse was raised on a free range, this is no longer the case. The breeding of this horse is now carried on in a similar way to breeding throughout North America and Europe. The rules, however, are still strict about returning an Icelandic horse to its homeland. It just isn't done. Once a horse leaves Iceland, she does not return.

The Icelandic horse is five-gaited—the walk, the trot, the canter, the pace, and the tolt. The four-beat tolt, or gait, is described as so smooth that riders demonstrate it by holding and not spilling a glass of water as they ride. The tolt itself can be slow or fast, as the rider wishes.

20

The Little Stone and Little Nag Horses

SHETLAND, HIGHLAND, AND WELSH

*T*he small, pretty pony among the wild, wind-lashed hills is so deeply etched in the collective memory that we have put the pony into a special place as a kindred spirit of childhood.

The romantic idea of the perfect pony is summed up by Olive Tilford Dargon *(The Welsh Pony)*:

> I climbed to the highest, craggiest hill in sight. On the top of it I found a small herd of ponies, living without bluff or boast the simple life. There were several mares with young foals, and some colts of poetic promise, which led me to press for entrance into the family circle; but with retreating dignity they let me know that I was a mere inquisitive bounder, and I was reduced to the old trick that used to work so successfully with the cows in the high meadow above the red cottage in Shelburne.
>
> I laid myself down, my hands over my eyes and my fingers craftily windowed, and in a few moments was surrounded by a group investigating me with scientific detachment. Then I found myself looking into eyes, very different. . . . I was admitted to a realm where it seemed for the moment, at least, that "beast, as man, had dreams/And sought his stars."

Do we remember, with the generous little pony's help, that we, too, long ago, careened the wind? Does the pony bring back this memory, wish, and dream? The time when, as the poet said, "Man was once a horse"?

History informs us that the nine ponies of the British Isles were each an indivisible group, with each breed having a unique and specialized character and appearance. Yet, as one, they shared what Elwyn Hartley Edwards *(The Encyclopedia of the Horse)* has termed "a constitutional strength, hardiness, and innate wisdom that are derived from their environment."

Man, environment, and pony stayed together for some twenty-five hundred years. Beginning in the Bronze Age, human beings had fastened themselves to this durable beast, but in the grand time of kings when Henry VIII reigned supreme, the little horse took a fall from grace. For it was Henry who, being much more particular about his horses than he was about his wives, passed the "Bill for the Breeding of Horses."

This document called for the extermination of "little stoned horses and nags of small stature and of little value be not only suffered to pasture thereupon but also to cover mares feeding there, whereof cometh in manner no profit or commodity."

All of which meant that equines below fourteen hands in height were killed or, in some cases, banished. Henry's edict would make England into the most horse-conscious nation in the world. Needless to say, the bigger, bolder breeds were capable of carrying heavy men, armored and laden with weaponry, whereas the little ponies could not.

Some poetical souls, in writing of this terrible time for the ponies, have suggested that many of them were spirited away by "Tells and Winkelrieds," to live in secrecy in the lofty hollows of the Welsh, Irish, and Scottish highlands.

Perhaps this is the time of magic when the ponies became associated with "little people." Certainly, like all animals under siege or threat of death, they knew of their fate and kept to the hills.

Today, something of this pony spell still exists, especially in the minds of our little people, our children. Ponies and pony carts are, for them, safe passage into the world of enchantment.

Many myths from the banishment period describe the pony as not only a carrier of magic, but also a spell-caster as well. The Scottish *kelpie*, for instance, is a creature of madness and danger, a water faerie that can change into a horse or a hairy man. The *kelpie* haunts rivers and streams, and after allowing an unsuspecting human to mount him, he might dash back into the water and give the rider a good—and sometimes dangerous—dunking.

In Ireland, the *aughisky* is a young horse of a far more diabolical nature. After carrying his victims into the water, he devours them, leaving nothing but their liver. *Aughiskies* inhabit seawater and live in lochs. Inland a rider is safe while riding them, but not so near the sea, where the smell or sight of salt air will spell the rider's death.

Folktales of dark horse spirits are balanced in the British Isles by tales of light, healing horses, too. One such animal in England was a workhorse that carted stones until they "broked his feet dreadful." The sand crack in his hoof was so wide you could put a finger in it. A blacksmith looking at it said he could do nothing for it as "fire that foot was."

The butcher was near at hand and had his ax ready, but the stone carter was proud of his horse. He took his horse to Wincanton where Saint Aloys gave the man a bit of cider, some bread, and cheese and swore the horse would soon be all right. It is said that the saint, who was also a smithy, removed the horse's bad leg and fixed it while the patient animal stood on three legs, nickering quietly and chewing a bit of hay. Soon the saint clapped on the mended leg with a 'Here we are then.'"

There is a carving of Saint Aloys in Wincanton Church and a fine alabaster in Nottingham Castle Museau representing the miracle. Nor is that the end of the myth, for it occurs even earlier in ancient Scandinavian folklore and involves the ride of Odin and Balder the Beautiful. This legend tells how Balder slipped and broke the leg, which Odin healed by tying a black thread with seven knots around the fracture. While so doing, he chanted this famous formula:

> *Baldur road. The foal slid.*
> *He lighted and he righted,*
> *Set joint to joint, bone to bone,*
> *Sinew to sinew,*
> *Heal in Odin's name.*

The spell and the poem have survived to modern times, but its Christian form has been altered to describe an accident during Christ's triumphal ride into Jerusalem.

> *The Lord rode. The foal slid.*
> *Set bone to bone,*
> *Sinew to sinew,*
> *Heal in the Holy Ghost's name.*

According to M. O. Howey *(The Horse in Magic and Myth)*, "Even today this spell is practiced in remote corners of the British Isles, not only on animals, but on human beings also, and apparently success still follows its use."

Incidentally, Balder the Beautiful appears as a foal, which could also be a pony; the Lord's mount, as we know, was an ass, an animal reminiscent of a pony. The same chant appears in Scotland in dialect form as

> *Our Lord rade, His foals foot slade:*
> *Down he lighted, His foals foot righted.*
> *Bone to bone, sinew to sinew.*
> *Blood to blood, flesh to flesh;*
> *Heal, in the name of the Father, Son, and Holy Ghost.*

The Greek centaur, Chiron, was half-man and half-horse and possessed great magic—medicinal plants and herbs as well as the art of surgery. Author Sharon Janus *(The Magic of Horses: Horses as Healers)* writes: "Dozens of mythological stories celebrate Chiron's impressive healing power. In one story, he performs surgery on a young Achilles whose ankle had been burned through magical practices. Chiron actually replaced Achilles' missing bone with a healthy one taken from a giant's skeleton."

Isn't this the seven-knotted gift of Odin? Saint Aloy's sacred anvil?

How well the ancient Greeks understood that horse and rider, joined as centaur, unified the disparate cosmos of the human and animal. The centaurs, it should be noted, added to chaotic adventures as well by chasing after mortal women, and it was the centaurs that accidentally brought about Chiron's death. Hercules was encircled by centaurs, and aiming a poison arrow at them, he mistakenly killed Chiron.

When the Greeks made man and horse one, they augmented the powers of each. No wonder then that Chiron is a planet of change, growth, and rebirth. It is the planet in astrology that has so much to do with the cycle of upheaval and renewal.

The Shetland pony, but for its size, looks like a workhorse. The coloration is variable: dark brown, red brown, black, and piebald. The winter coat grows very shaggy, and the summer coat is sleek and short. According to Dorothy Childs Hogner *(The Horse Family)*, the life of this work animal mirrors its people:

> Many people of the Shetland Islands live in one-room stone houses. They burn peat to keep their houses warm. They use the island ponies to bring the peat from the pits. One small pony can carry as much as 140 pounds on his back at one time. Sometimes the pony lives with the people in the same house. Now and then the owner feeds his pony a little hay or a few fish heads but the pony finds most of its food for itself. It grazes on the island. Though there is little good grass, the Shetland keeps strong.

This was written nearly fifty years ago, yet much of it still applies. An old Shetland proverb states, "An Orkney man is a farmer who has to fish; a Shetland man is a fisherman who has to farm." Proof of this may be found today in the nets made of horse's manes and tails. In fact, one of the earliest laws recorded in Shetland warned would-be thieves not to cut "any other man's horse tail or mane, under the pain of ten pounds," so the Shetland pony bridged the gulf between two ways of life—that of the farm and the foam, so to say.

The pony and the people were also of a mixed breed, British and Viking, the one to the south and the other to the north. The British hill-type pony is thus found in the Shetland, as is a Norse breed that contains some Asian blood. An early representation in art is a ninth-century stone carving from the island of Bressay showing a hooded priest riding a very small pony.

The exact origin of the Shetland has long been a mystery. No matter how they came to these isolated islands, they had to cope with hostile wind, bad grass, hard ground, and a climate that stole body heat like the proverbial thief in the night. Thus came the short-limbed, short-backed, thick-necked, big-eared, unbreakable, keenly intelligent, foaled-in-the-fields pony.

The Shetland pony's flowing mane and tail, furry winter coat, and surefooted, flowing, long-striding gait are all inbred traits, wrought from a steep island where the poor grazing forced the little horse to cover uneven miles to get its sustenance. Common grazing, or *scattald*, as it was known on the Shetland Islands, was a way to supplement acres of rough-heather moorland. Both the Shetland pony and Shetland sheep have survived where other stock could not.

Off the *scattalds* the ponies were used to *flitting the peats*, which meant a cross-country trek in probable bad weather while lugging heavy woven saddlebags. These *kishies*, so called, were hung from wooden *klibbers*, a kind of saddle frame. Most crofters did not ride Shetlands, and so the little horses remained pack-and-saddle animals for most of their history.

After the coming of roads, they became draft ponies until the Mines Act of 1847 prevented children from working as miner's helpers in the British Isles. As the Shetlands could travel down the narrowest shafts and carry the heaviest loads, they were considered ideal for underground labor. Loyalty between horse and man ran deep in the pits, and many lives were saved by a balking or bolting pony. The sad truth, though, is that the miners went aboveground at the end of the day, but the horses remained underground all the time.

In Great Britain, ponies were still in the mines as late as the 1970s. The mining industry also affected the quality of breed stock on the islands. Local crofters exported the "best and stoutest" stallions. So subsistence farmers had very little good-sized stock. The big landowners, however, sold fillies to America, where the demands from stud farms were high.

Before the 1920s, English royalty kept Shetlands, thus making them popular with the upper-class children in Britain. After that, the Welsh pony became the pony of choice for riding and the internal combustion engine replaced the Shetland as society's workhorse, drying up the market for the sale of Shetland ponies.

Today the pony has made a comeback, and the Shetland is now holding its own in the showring as well as being a popular choice for children and families. At home on the islands, they're still grazing on the side of the road, looking wild, but a proud possession of a local crofter.

There is so much magic in the collective pony that one might wonder if this little horse is imprisoned in childhood fantasies or if there is another reason for its unaccountability as a "real" animal. Mythically, little horses have often been the ones that carried special powers, like the horse effigies from Africa, Ireland, and Native America that could fit into the palm of your hand.

The question with the pony is, did we make the myth to match the pony, or was it the other way around? The abundance of myths link the little horse with the unicorn. Perhaps, as some say, the pony is really the unicorn minus the horn.

In many of our most fanciful tales, the little horse can fly, thus giving it the quality of the half-griffin, the hippogriff. This fabled creature was part-horse, part-lion, and part-eagle. The only horse parts that showed were the feet and the plumed tail.

There is an old nursery rhyme that explains why British royal crests feature the lion and unicorn, but it does not tell us anything about the hippogriff except maybe this: There is a desire for all opposites to attract, and this is as true in mythology as in reality.

> *The lion and unicorn were fighting for the crown;*
> *The lion beat the unicorn all around the town.*
> *Some gave them white bread and some gave them brown;*
> *Some gave them plum cake and drummed them out of town.*

Aside from the narwhal and the rhino, the unicorn, though imaginary, is singular in our bestiary literature. The creature started out with the head and body of a horse, the tail of a lion, the beard of a goat, the hind legs of an antelope, and the horn of a narwhal-rhino.

The horn itself is of specific importance because it was in ancient times thought to be an antidote against any kind of poison. Horns, by the way, are still widely used as fertility potions in Asia.

The other known magical property of the unicorn was how it came to be tamed. Only when in the presence of a maiden would it become completely tractable and place its horned head in her lap.

Spanish poet Federico García Lorca weaves a gypsy spell around the horse-unicorn connection in his poem "The Comical History of Don Pedro, Knight." Here the unicorn is like the soul of the horse.

> Over the flat highway
> Two women and one old man
> Carrying silver lamps
> To the graveyard wend their way.
> In the saffron there they find
> Don Pedro's black horse dead.
> The afternoon's secret voice
> Plaintive, whines to the sky.
> Absence, a unicorn,
> Shatters his crystal horn.

The old belief that little ponies can be fully appreciated only by little children survives today. And it's not, as we would think, because of their size, their childlike quality, but rather their incorruptible goodness. Little do we know, as they say, because when a real horse is not available, children frequently retreat into the world of their imaginations, where unicorns and ponies of all colors thrive on the antic hay of fantasy.

As Michael J. Rosen (Horse People: Writers and Artists on the Horses They Love) writes of horse lover Candyce Barnes: "What other creature so preoccupies us in our youth? When no real horse fulfilled Candyce Barnes's girlhood wish each Christmas, she 'created Phantom, who lived in my room, accompanied me everywhere, and ate off my plate during dinner (like me, Phantom hated chicken pot pie and English peas).'"

The Characteristics of the Ponies of the British Isles

The Shetland pony comes in all colors, most commonly black, chestnut, gray, bay dun, and blue roan. The Welsh Pony and Cob Society do not allow piebald and skewbald. This smallest of the British pony breeds has a maximum height of forty-two inches and a minimum of twenty-eight inches. The coat is thick with a heavy mane and tail, which protects against harsh weather.

The Highland pony, or *garron*, was traditionally used in the crofts as a pack/work animal. It is one of the oldest pony breeds in the Isles, dating back to the eighth century B.C.—and the *only* pony in the British Isles to have the dorsal stripe and zebra legs, dun color, and black mane and tail that indicate primitive origins. This is a heavily built pony, usually about fourteen to fifteen hands.

The Welsh pony carries Arabian blood and was even called a miniature Arab in the 1800s; it's a riding pony that retains the character and temperament of the Welsh mountain pony. It stands around thirteen hands and comes in all colors, but the most common tends to be gray. There are four breed types, the Welsh mountain A, B, C, and D. The last two types are the Welsh cob crosses. The last three derive from the first, the Welsh mountain pony.

The Welsh pony is perhaps the most popular pony breed in the world. Even so, when you see these surefooted ponies on the hills of Wales, there is a flickery wildness about them that is long remembered. Moreover, when they see you staring at them, their ears twitch, their tails whisk, and then they fly off like a many-coated cloud to hover well away from human eyes, far off on the humpbacked hills.

21

The Fisherman's Horse

CONNEMARA PONY

The only native breed on the Emerald Isle, the Connemara, goes back to the Celts, some twenty-five hundred years ago. This adaptable animal was a hauler of war chariots and carts and a strong mount for the tribal warriors of the magic island who once held sway over so much of the known world. Today, it is hard to believe that on this little pony's back rested the fate of nations.

Legend tells us that when the Spanish Armada sank, the horses, undoubtedly Barbs, swam to shore and bred with the native Connemara, which increased the pony's size and made it the largest of the small breeds.

Coincidentally, there is another myth that explains the Manx cat's origin in the same way—supposedly, it, too, slipped off the sinking armada.

As much as anything else, the rocky, barren, mountainous landscape helped to shape the Connemara. It forged it into a cold-resistant, agile, adaptable, surefooted animal. Another shaper of the horse's destiny was the pounding, permanently wrinkled Irish coastline.

To survive, the horse had to be a good jumper, load carrier, racer, dragger (it even hauled seaweed used as fertilizer), and all-around barn companion. In 1897, Professor Ewart of Edinburgh, as part of a royal commission that was examining horse breeding in Ireland, said, "The Connemara was strong and hardy as a mule . . . fertile and free from disease . . . capable of living where all but wild ponies would starve."

Connemara owner and writer Karen D. Rickenbach writes of her favorite horse, Sir William's Irish Taffy. Her personal story explains why the breed is noted for its rugged wisdom on the shrouded trail.

When I opened the old barn door, Taffy abruptly stopped chewing her sweet oats and greeted me with a stare of surprise. It was bitterly cold outside, and when I kissed her warm muzzle, she flared her wide black nostrils, pressing a sweet equine breath onto my face. During colder months she grew a grayish dapple winter coat with tiny white spots resembling miniature half-moons. A stunning Connemara Pony with dreamy brown eyes and a strong chiseled face, all of Taffy's points were black and she had a broken white star on her forehead. Sometimes I traced the outline of the star with my finger, telling her it was shaped like the little Emerald Isle.

As I slipped the bit between her teeth, I thought of how often I'd felt her tough bloodline under me, the centuries-old strength, from ancestors who roamed the hillsides and moors of Ireland. When we rode out of the stable, it was into a world of icicles and wintry branches. The day was eerily silent. Across the barren potato field, the Sagaponack Woods looked like a magnificent white castle. Approaching it, I thought, *How will we get into the snowy dome?* Even the bridle paths were blocked by thick snowy doors. But I urged Taffy on. It was all one whiteness—the ground, the sky, and as far as we could see. Taffy kept her black-rimmed ears pricked at attention.

Once in the woods Taffy pushed through the wall of snow without hesitation. Instantly we were in another world. Inside, the woods became a glass menagerie. Icicles like long cones of diamonds glittered in the sun that was peeking through. Mounds of rock-solid snow, like tiny glaciers, mirrored them. Taffy's eyes were wide with curiosity and she was thrilled by the free reins that I gave her. Into narrow passageways we went, wondering where they'd lead. For a while, we were both amazed by the white maze that surrounded us, but in time I found that we were traveling in circles and half-circles, and going nowhere in the blowing snow. The temperature had dropped and with it came more wind gusts and more snow. Some Canadian geese honked overhead, their cries signaling the end of day. Then I realized that several hours must have passed without my knowing it. Dusk was approaching, and if we didn't get out of the snow dome before nightfall, we would be in real trouble.

Taffy sensed my nervousness and switched her tail. I looked for a familiar tree, a sign of something I had seen before, yet there were only cascades of snow. At once I became desperate, fearful. I turned Taffy around and started another way—we went nowhere. We were both totally lost. Looking again for a sign, I saw an omen—a Snowy Owl. I thought, *Maybe the owl is an angel who will lead us out of the maze.* It cocked its wide heart-shaped face, so alive with gleaming golden eyes. My frozen saddle creaked under me. Taffy stood quite still. She too felt the owl's presence. She seemed tense with suspicion. I stared at the owl, so serene in its plush feather cloak.

For a moment the three of us were locked in stillness. The owl's claws were perfect black knots wrapped tightly around the dark branch. I wished it would fly like a shepherd in the direction of our escape, but the owl sat quiet, its burning yellow eyes seeming to go through us. What was it thinking?

Suddenly the owl lifted a wing, and I took this gesture as a message to go towards the south. I nudged Taffy to proceed in that direction, and presently we came to another solid wall of snow. I turned in my saddle to regard the owl, but it had flown to another tree. Or had it? I hadn't heard its wings flapping. . . . Had it really flown? Was the owl tricking us? I looked at it carefully, and the creature offered only a cold, inquisitive stare. Then I realized the owl wasn't magic, nor was it a shepherd. Despite its rarity and splendor, it was neither a trickster nor a savior, but only an owl in a winter tree. And Taffy and I were still lost.

Now I urged Taffy to face the snow wall that was directly in front of us. Bowing her head, she pushed right through it. Then as if walking on a frozen pond she put one hoof in front of the other and walked into yet another door of snow. Once again it broke before her head and she pushed a clear passage in front of us. Now she was leading the way and I was the respectful follower. As the darkness settled around us, Taffy became all the more spirited. The trail was surely underfoot when I made out my friend Patsy's little house. That was when I thanked Taffy's strong ancestral spirits: Canrower Boy, Sir William's Tammy, Bridge Boy, Kiss-Me-Kate, Camus John, and

> Little Mo for making possible the miracle of my special pony,
> Sir William's Irish Taffy.

As Rickenbach has pointed out, horses give confidence to human beings in more ways than compass points and orientation on the trail. Her horse Taffy understood her innermost thoughts and feelings. Some of these are related to healing the troubled heart. Horse owner and writer Sharon Janus speaks about how the horse can be an effective medium for the resolution of unsettled human emotions. The Emily Griffith Center in Larkspur, Colorado, where there are "60 young men, ages 10 through 19; sixteen equine therapists; one human therapeutic riding instructor, Cindy Sharp; and a number of doctors, psychologists, cooks, and counselors" provide Equine Facilitated Psychotherapy.

The facility shelters young men with learning and emotional difficulties as well as sexual-abuse and court-ordered crime cases.

According to Janus, "The sixteen equine therapists and Cindy are instrumental to healing as well as in teaching alternatives to better ways of being and acting in society. Cindy specifically calls on horses not only to heal the boys' emotional injuries, but to lay a foundation for basic skills that they'll need for the rest of their lives."

The basic belief, centered on the Western work ethic that "the horse is a partner in work and in play," adds a dimension of fellowship and cooperative training that the residents have, in many cases, not experienced this way before.

One of the things that Sharon observed firsthand at the Griffith Center was the immediate bond that can take place between a human and an animal. Horses, she says, are noted for their honesty; they tell you how they feel at every step of the way. Therefore, when a youth expresses doubt about dealing with feelings frankly, the horse is there—through plaintive action—to show the necessity of being honest and direct.

One resident writes of the immediacy of the horse's affection: "Face the Sun put his head down on my shoulder and rested it there, then picked up his head and licked my cheek. I was so happy that I started to cry. Face the Sun was the first animal to show that much love toward me. I said 'I love you' to Face, and gave him a big hug."

Sharon also says that the opposite of this, mistrustful feelings, can also be shown and can be made effective as a teaching tool. Some Nevada mustangs are used in this regard because, unlike other horses at the center, they "demonstrate that they don't trust humans since they weren't born and raised with them."

In the course of their stay at the center, residents learn to ride, rope, and work on a horse—all skills that parallel human work relations in almost any given situation. Horses show patience and unconditional friendship in addition to honesty, camaraderie, and cooperativeness. Two-legged therapists can go only so far. The magic comes from four-legged healers whose message goes straight to the heart.

The Characteristics of the Connemara Pony

The body of the Connemara pony, compact and deep, is not bulky. These horses have short legs, and, in fact, it has been said that although they "stand on short legs, they cover a lot of ground."

They stand between twelve and fourteen hands, making them one of the largest pony breeds; however, they compete in events that much bigger horses enter, and the little Connemara always does well. Indeed, she is an excellent hunter and jumper.

The Connemara has a good sloping shoulder and moves freely with little knee action. The head is handsome, with a well-defined jaw and good width between large, kindly eyes. Noted for being easy keepers and not requiring expensive rations, the Connemara is a family horse, good-natured and user-friendly.

Originally dun in color, you rarely find this so-called primitive shade any more because it has been replaced with gray, black bay, and brown. Black points are common; paints are considered unacceptable.

22

The Horse of the River Clyde

CLYDESDALE

lthough the Clydesdale has been around for about 150 years, it is today the most visible and influential heavy horse of draft stock in the world.

The Select Clydesdale Horse Society began in 1883, founded by two breeders—Lawrence Drew and his friend David Riddell—who were committed to improving the bloodline by not allowing shire mares to breed with Clydesdales. This was in direct opposition to the official Clydesdale Horse Society studbook, but they did not care and went ahead with their program, and it is a good thing they did.

Among draft horses the Clydesdale is noted for flamboyant style and bold, flashy spirit. No wonder, too, that the early bloodstock was imported from Flemish great horses, the true ancestors of the modern draft horse. This was one of the only equines capable of carrying a ponderous knight in ironclad armor.

How, you might ask, did the name Clydesdale come about?

Well, a certain duke of Hamilton brought six black Flemish stallions to the fertile dale along the River Clyde, in Lanarkshire, Scotland, in the early eighteenth century.

From this original breed stock, the offspring were known as Clydesman's horses, which, in time, was abbreviated to Clydesdales. Later on, when Scottish farmers emigrated into Canada, they brought their Clydesdales with them, and after this, at about the time of the Civil War, these same farmers went south into the United States, and, once again, the great horse was drawn into the machinery of war.

Still later, the hauling ability of the Clydesdale, along with its adaptable, tractable manner, made it not only the choice of farmers, but also a good pick for the increasingly popular brewery business. Thus did Clydesdales endear themselves to the Anheuser-Busch family as delivery-wagon horses. In fact, they seemed to grow famous together.

How this came to pass is a unique piece of Americana—and who can say how much of it is legend and how much is fact, for the two are quite intertwined.

It all starts with Adolphus Busch, a German immigrant who married Lily Anheuser. Adolphus took over his father-in-law's brewery business in St. Louis and quickly made it one of the most successful in the United States.

Naturally, Adolphus knew that one of the essential ingredients in moving vast amounts of beer was the horse—horses, actually—well-fed, well-treated horses.

When Busch erected a stable to house his draft horses, people said, "It isn't a stable, it's an Equine Palace." This made him happy. So did brewing. And he passed his love of the brewery and its powerful horses on to his son, August, who, in turn, passed it on to his son, August Jr.

By 1919 the beer was flowing and the horses were tramping, and the business was never better. Then came Prohibition. And with it, the gas-driven delivery truck.

Either of these could have spelled the end of the Busch beer dynasty. But, curiously, they did not. Time intervened. The great horses snorted impatiently to make their rounds. But August Jr. held on for all he was worth.

And, just as the great horses of Flemish knights went back to the fields where they were raised after the wars were over, so, too, did August keep his field horses occupied as he made a meager living by selling yeast, corn, and malt syrup. Fourteen years later, Prohibition was done. August Jr. smiled, for he knew that beer was going to be in very great demand—and so, he decided, would be his great outdated steeds!

He had, in fact, a deep longing for the days of his childhood, when his father's massive horses were not only beautiful to watch parading down the tree-lined avenues of St. Louis, but were absolutely necessary to the transport of beer barrels. In 1933, of course, this would not be the case. The ever-present Ford truck was available for this purpose. However, August Jr. had a seditious, delicious secret, which he kept to himself. Slyly, he bought eight Clydesdales and tack in Chicago. These he kept hidden, shrouded in secrecy, in an unused brewery stable.

On April 7, 1933, the first beer in fourteen years flowed brightly out of the Busch spigots into barrels. That same day, August Jr. walked into his father's office and invited him to look at the new car he had just purchased.

Obligingly, August Sr. followed his son outside into the sunlight. There, squinting in the sun, he was astonished at what greeted him.

There was an impressive six-horse Clydesdale team pulling a big red beer wagon. It was an image from the past, burnished beautifully and fashioned into a dream of the present moment.

And that was how a world-famous, thirst-quenching symbol was born. A logo that is still used today—the great, proud beer horses of Anheuser-Busch stomping down the green-leafed streets of summer and clomping through the frosty landscapes of snowy winter.

Yet it was August Jr.'s imagination that carried these simple, effective, nostalgic, mythical and mythmaking horses out to the forefront of the nation. Without hesitation, he shipped the Clydesdales by train to New York City, where they were unloaded and hitched to their red- and gold-trimmed wagon.

Al Smith, the former governor of New York, was astonished as the horse-and-wagon team trotted noisily up to his house to deliver two cases of beer—a grand reminder that he had helped to repeal Prohibition.

Nor did August Jr. stop there. His dream dancers went forth, in full regalia, to Washington, D.C., where they paraded up Pennsylvania Avenue, stopping at the White House. Here the horses caused quite a stir as another case of beer was hand delivered. This one went to President Franklin D. Roosevelt.

Today, this bit of modern mythmaking lives on.

And the Anheuser-Busch Clydesdales, which make more than three hundred appearances each year, have been on the road ever since the "gift horses" of the 1930s.

The earliest mention of the Clydesdale occurs in a Celtic myth. The warriors of Fionn find this great light-colored, tangled-coated horse, and they are so surprised by his size that they order him around by spear point—or they *try* to do this, at any rate.

These tough Celts saw themselves as first-rate horsemen, but they met their match with the tangle-coated horse.

To begin with, the animal was so large and ungainly that, on first seeing him, Fionn's men try to best him as a beast of the forest.

> Cunnaun seized the boar-spear and hurled himself down the hill slope. Soon he was thrusting terribly at the tangle-coated horse: thrusts that would have been gashes and deathly wounds to him, but the point slid off and left the beast unhurt—not a thrust of them all knocked a hair out of his side! Cunnaun gathered his strength for one mighty thrust. The spear point slid from that shaggy shoulder and glanced along the bony ribs: it did not even leave a scratch there! It just seemed to tickle the yellow horse, for he stopped snapping and kicking and turned round to look at Cunnaun. He winked at him first with one eye and then he winked with the other eye and all the while he smiled, and smiled, 'til his face was nothing but a smile. Cunnaun hit him one last resounding smack, and the boar-spear fell in two halves.

This is a shape-shifting myth, where "the tangled mat of ugliness miscalled a horse" is changed into a lovely silver equine, the likes of which has never been seen by Fionn's men.

In the shape-shifting horse, the old sea gods of Dahna are united forever with the warrior-hunters of earthy Ireland. This power of unification, as in a national song or poem, is what makes mythology sacred rather than secular history.

So the earth-sea realms coming together bring about even more changes on the human scene—we have a subsequent merging of animals and men, gods and men. By combining forces in this way, people become godlike, while distant gods turn friendly and, sometimes, even mortal. What results is a brotherly, sisterly nation of godlike beings, who can also change into animals . . . ah, Ireland.

In the center of this psychic circus of the soul, if you will, is the huge, stone-footed horse, which can, in the wink of an eye, go silver and travel about the air like a dragonfly. The bardic echo sung by Diarmid sounds joking and skeptical.

> A horse so nice
> You kick him twice
> Before he moves.
> A horse with hooves
> Like water vats.
> He has an ear that flops
> A high backbone that drops
> A tail for switching flies
> He can't run when he tries,
> Bald Cunnaun's horse.

Ah, but when he changes, how the man changes his tune!

More than any other, this charming Gaelic tale requires a certain suspension of disbelief, a love of mischief and beauty, playfulness and poetry. It is what the Clydesdale is all about, too. Perhaps the moral might be: Do not judge a horse by its tangled cover or its great size, for what lies underneath is the silkiest of magical spells.

The Characteristics of the Clydesdale

Because the Clydesdale has become an example of a showy draft horse, his physical characteristics are very specific. It is claimed that this fine equine possesses quality and weight without grossness and bulk. The horse stands from sixteen to eighteen hands and can weigh as much as two thousand pounds. Some of the older stallions and geldings are even taller and can weigh up to twenty-two hundred pounds. Each horse has exceptional feet and limbs with long, silky hair below the knees. The hocks draw special attention to the feet when the Clydesdale starts into that famous, springy trot.

The head is broad, and the front of the face is flat, with neither a dished nor a Roman nose. Clydesdales are noted for having a bright, clear eye. The most common colors are bay, black, and brown; also some roans, with occasional chestnuts.

The Clydesdale has become increasingly popular as a pleasure horse. From the more compactly built equines of the 1920s and 1930s, today's draft horse is taller and smoother-gaited.

23

The Blooded Running Horse

THOROUGHBRED

T he Thoroughbred is known for his racing ability, but is equally well known, in some circles, for his skill in fox-hunting, show jumping, and dressage. Predominant, though, is the Thoroughbred's influence on the world horse population. No single breed has had more impact on other breeds than the Thoroughbred, and this is due to careful, scientific breeding over the centuries.

Three horses of the East are thought to make up the Thorough-bred's background. They are the Byerly Turk, the Darley Arabian, and the Godolphin Arabian. But these three do not include, and should, the classic English racing stock that was culled and created by royalty to produce a base of excellent stud stock. The first royal patron of horse racing in England was Henry VIII, who, in charac-teristic fashion, went in for it whole hog, or whole *horse*, as it should be said, despite the pope's demands for cessation of all racing in England.

Founder of the Royal Paddocks at Hampton Court, Henry knew no bounds in anything he loved or hated, and he eventually stabled a thousand horses of Barb-influenced bloodlines, which he brought in from Spain and Italy, as well as stabling native equines such as the Fell pony descendent, the Galloway of northern England. He also encouraged the breeding of the Irish hobby, the ancestor of the Connemara.

The earliest horse races were not English, though. They originated in the Middle East, where falconing and gazelle hunting were most popular. Hunting and racing were brothers, as it were—manly pur-suits, afield and afun.

The hunting of ibex can be seen today on a fifth-century Persian plate of silver and gold, and equine races appear as well on painted Greek vases from about 500 B.C.

Which comes first, the chariot race or the horse race? It is believed to be the former. As we know, kings competed for the prize—a gar-land of wild olive—but the first recorded mounted race was at the Olympic Games in 624 B.C. Here, the traditional olive garland was, depending upon the male or female point of view, upgraded or downgraded to a slave woman.

Thus the stakes have been selectively raised—and lowered—over the past two thousand years.

In 1693 William Penn, the founder of Pennsylvania, said, "Men are more careful about the breeding of their horses . . . than the breeding of their children."

This truth holds true today, but right from the start, horse racing involved large crowds, big bets, and fierce brawls—all to determine the usually outrageous and often ambiguous results. Indeed, racing involved—*required* might be a better word—a certain amount of cheating as well.

Big money and big horses, fast money and faster horses have been the rules to follow. Even during chariot-racing days, the star drivers needed bodyguards and food tasters to keep them from harm. Today, the average jockey needs just a little bit of food, a bone-spare body made of feathers, and a very, very fast horse.

Ironically, the ancient Greeks believed that horse racing made for a healthy body and for excellent longevity. However, as the "sport of kings," it frequently bankrupted the rich and elevated the poor—hence its enormous popularity. This, then, is the myth of the Thoroughbred—the turning of a pauper into a prince, not overnight, but in the blink of an eye.

Starting with Queen Elizabeth in the sixteenth century, women got into the riding and the racing forum. The Virgin Queen rode until late in life. Queen Isabella started riding when she was three years old. Queen Victoria was an adept rider in her youth, but she gave it up in her later—certainly not *wilder* but *wider*—years.

Horsewomen generally rode sidesaddle. This began in Europe as a distinction of class, a definition between upper and lower. Riding *pillion*, it was called, which meant sitting on a pad. However, ancient cultures believed that naked riding was good for childbearing.

In America, horse racing took off, so to speak, almost at once, with an English racetrack in the state of Virginia. According to Milton

Meltzer *(Hold Your Horses)*, the purse included "40,000 in gold, hogsheads of tobacco, bolts of cloth and silver plate." Horse racing in the South started out as upper class and ended up sort of democratic, with black jockeys as the rule throughout the nineteenth century. The Irish lower classes made horse racing popular in the North, however. A former prizefighter, John Morrissey, helped to found the track at Saratoga Springs, New York.

Blooded horses dominated all of the events so-named because no horse but a Thoroughbred could go faster or more beautifully at a fast speed. Our best American myths come from the racetrack, or from the mythos of the track, anyway. Such tales usually revolve around high-stakes gambling and the rags-to-riches theme.

But what makes the myth of the horse race both good and true, whether fact or fiction, is that the underrated horse and the small-pocketed bettor could always wind up on the winning side. This is the American Dream in well-muscled action.

An archetypal tale of the track is the true story of Lil E. Tee.

Lil E. Tee was a colt with a dime-store pedigree born on a Pennsylvania farm in 1989. Suffering from an immune deficiency disease and a bad case of colic that required surgery, he was sold for $3,000.

Overcoming these sorry beginnings, Tee went on to become the 17-to-1 long shot at Churchill Downs for the Kentucky Derby, the most prestigious horse race in recent history. True to form, and true to the American Dream, E.T.'s win was a fairy tale come true.

He ran against Arazi, the favorite, who had drawn a celebrity crowd of film stars and sheiks, all expecting to see their charmed Thoroughbred surpass Secretariat's Derby record.

What happened is history, and well told by John Eisenberg *(The Longest Shot: Lil E. Tee and the Kentucky Derby)*.

> Suddenly, the fastest of them all, supposedly, began rallying from the back of the pack. Arazi was making his move. The famous favorite had fallen far behind early, running dead last

under the wire on the front stretch, then seventeenth through the turn and into the backstretch. . . . Racing four wide, he began to put away horses in a dazzling rush.

Goodbye Mr. Devious. Goodbye My Luck Runs North. Goodbye Ecstatic Ride. Goodbye Thyer. Goodbye West by West. Goodbye Disposal. Arazi was flying. He went by E.T. like a shot. . . .

Half a dozen lengths back, amid the obscurity of the horses destined for the middle and back of the pack, E.T. began chasing the leaders. . . . Arazi had passed thirteen horses in a half-mile. But there was a problem, the Derby was almost two furlongs longer than the Juvenile.

Pat Day was among the first to notice that Arazi was starting to slow down. "He had opened up about four lengths on me pretty quick after passing me," Day said later. "But I kept my eyes on him, and when we went into the turn he wasn't pulling away. In fact I started closing ground."

. . . Day brought the charging E.T. up to Arazi's heels. The hardscrabble, long shot son of At the Threshold, turned down for auction, sold three times, finally met the silver-spoon favorite worth millions. It was no contest. Day paused for several strides, then swept E.T. around Valenzuela and the tiring chestnut. Goodbye Arazi.

After a hairline fracture in a leg, E.T. was retired to stud, and he impregnated fifty mares in his first year. Jim Plemmons, owner of Pine Oak Lane Farm, says, "Whether he'll be a great sire, only time will tell, but with his natural speed and conformation, we fully expect him to be a good sire. Maybe some people don't believe it. But then, people have underestimated this horse since the first day of his life."

One thing that is never underestimated in the avid literature of Thoroughbred racing is the synchronic rhythm of the horse, as estimated by the spectator's eye or, better yet, the jockey's poetical memory. From jockeys come an economy of phrase commensurate with the flight of hooves. Mystery writer Dick Francis speaks of this in "Paperback Rider," from Michael J. Rosen's *Horse People: Writers and Artists on the Horses They Love:* "I could still feel the way I'd moved with the horse, the ripple of muscle through both the striving bodies, uniting in one. I could still feel the irons round my feet, the calves of my legs gripping, the balance, the nearness to my head of the stretching brown neck, the blowing in my mouth, my hands on the reins. . . ."

Perhaps, ultimately, it is this thrill beyond imagining or even hearing that is shared by viewer, bettor, and even reader, a feeling that crosses the line of human and animal psyche into the realm of myth: "Give me a horse to ride and a race to ride in and I don't care if I wear silks or pajamas. I don't care if there's anyone watching or not. I don't care if I don't earn much money or break my bones or if I have to starve to keep my weight down. All I care about is riding and racing and winning if I can" (*Bonecrack* by Dick Francis).

This from a man, a jockey-writer, a writer's jock, who, at seventy-seven, interviewer Franz Lidz says, looks as trim and tough as a "hawthorne staff," not bad for a fellow "who's broken a fair number of bones in his body above the waist: skull, wrist, arm, and three vertebrae." In horse and man, it is not adrenaline, nor fever, nor training alone—though all of these things might be part of it—that goads the heart and drives the mind past pain to be loosed from the earth at last. Having let go gravity's embrace, horse and rider find a place all their own, a separate peace known only to the airborne—to astronauts, poets, and dreamers floating free in the star-streamed turf of space.

Edna Ferber *(Giant)* describes the archetypal Thoroughbred, My Mistake, which is a fitting name for the horse that throws and kills Luz in the novel. Luz—portrayed by Mercedes McCambridge in the film—is a lusty cowgirl who has it in for the horse as well as her owner, Leslie Lynnton, played by Elizabeth Taylor.

Ferber describes My Mistake as "a satin-coated sorrel . . . long of leg, neat of hoof, long muscular neck, deep chest. Her hoofs seemed scarcely to touch the ground; they flicked the earth as delicately as a ballet dancer's toes."

In the novel she is a filly; in the film, a stallion. But no matter—she/he is all Thoroughbred.

When Bick Benedict (Rock Hudson) rides "the little filly, she jerked her head to glare at him with rolling resentful eyeballs, she skittered sideways. She gave him a nasty five minutes." Bick's sister, Luz, is not so fortunate with her ride. She is thrown and killed, and the beautiful horse is put down as a result.

However, without the plot-perfect event of Luz's death, Jett Rink (James Dean), her sort of adopted surrogate son, wouldn't have become a billionaire, which is the point of the novel and the film. Jett's oil money turns the rough old cattle range into a playground for the rich.

Jett, in the opening scenes of *Giant*, is good-natured with the spunky Thoroughbred, and all animals, though he is coy and suspicious around people. This was quite true of Dean in real life. He adored cats, cattle, dogs, and especially horses.

Giant topped James Dean's meteoric rise as an actor, and it made him internationally known even though he died shortly before it was finished, and his friend Nick Adams did voice-overs to complete the last scene.

The satiny Thoroughbred from *Giant* was already a star of television. Better known as Fury, after the Saturday afternoon series of the same name starring Peter Graves and William Fawcett, this Thoroughbred began life as Highland Dale on a Missouri farm. Fury was twenty-six months old when he appeared in the film classic *Black Beauty*, and his name changed often from picture to picture—Highland Dale, Beauty, Gypsy, Fury, and probably others as well. In real life, Fury suffered from heaves, which are similar to asthma. Dusty hay is the cause most often cited for this disease, but we wonder if he didn't also suffer from overexposure to "lights, camera, action."

The Characteristics of the Thoroughbred

The true key to the Thoroughbred's greatness is the speed and endurance that made him the popular choice of horsemen, polo players, foxhunters, jumpers, and show people.

The Thoroughbred stands a little over an average of sixteen hands, and his Arabian ancestry is revealed in the refined head and widely spaced, intelligent eyes. His neck might be long and light, with high and well-defined withers and a deep chest. The legs are long and clean, but the hips and thighs are well muscled. Coat colors might be bay, dark bay, chestnut, black, or gray. Roans are rare. White markings are frequently seen on the faces and legs of all Thoroughbreds.

24

The Great Horse

BELGIAN

fox.

T he great black horses of the Middle Ages came from Belgium. This was no era for an unmettlesome steed. Many wicked lords, as the tales of Lancelot reveal, seized a sizable horse and thundered their way to freedom. Mythologically, there was always a horse, always an escape, and ever a battle in which to be boldly seated upon a saddlebow or dangerously unhorsed in the blink of an eye.

In those bad, bold old days, enchantments *were* enchantments, and horses cast a huge shadow on the green sward of literature, if not history. To be sure, life was tentative, actions were not. But the whole thing, chivalry, was quite silly. Men fought like lions and died like dogs. And in reality, horses were neither godly nor great; they were like machinery. Still, in our mythology, there *were* godly horses, ones that outshone the real rank-and-file equines of the Middle Ages.

In true battles the horse was the platform upon which the man carried lance or sword. If the horse was good, the knight's sword was well forged, and his heart was pure, such a man might—with God's grace—live just a little bit longer.

The following passage comes from a thirteenth-century Arthurian manuscript that appears in *Dolorous Gard: Chronicles of King Arthur* by Andrea Hopkins:

> For the new knight was strong and swift and he fought like a lion. The first knight to emerge from the castle he impaled through the body with his lance, leaving him dead on the ground. The second he unhorsed and broke his arm. The third knight was dispatched by a massive blow over the helm; the fourth was borne out of his saddle by the lance and, falling directly in front of the new knight, was trampled to death under his horse's hooves.

So, in all ways and woes, in every valor and dolor, the horse was vastly present in the high Middle Ages, and the Belgian supplied the genetic iron from which all the modern draft breeds would later be forged. Stallions from Belgium were exported to many parts of Europe, but no equines came into Belgium, so that the fixed breed type was standardized and made firm.

By 1891, however, the exportation of Belgian stock had spread to Russia, Italy, Germany, France, and the old Austro-Hungarian Empire.

Although Belgian horse types were known to exist in western Europe in the time of Caesar, they became concretized in the words of medieval writers as the "great horses."

In time the breed and the place of its origin became a kind of ancestral home for the great horse wherein an international showcase was established and stallions were given certified conformation. A system of district shows culminated in the great national show in Brussels.

Decade after decade, the number of horses that left Belgium for breeding purposes increased. The American Belgian Association was founded in 1897 in Wabash, Indiana, and the breed offices are still there. From the turn of the century, the Belgian became more popular, and lively controversy over the best American draft horse—the most utilitarian draft for America—inflamed the owners of Percheron, Clydesdale, and shire, all of which enjoyed a substantial lead in this country.

The draft horse declined in popularity in the 1920s. Yet, ironically, the Belgian moved into a very solid number two position, and its decline was much less than other breeds. By the mid-1930s, even though America was suffering from the Great Depression, there was a dramatic upturn in draft-horse fortunes. The importation of horses from Belgium assumed record proportions.

According to Belgian horse breeders and historians, it was World War II that nearly ended European draft-horse breeding. A number of factors contributed to this, among them the German invasion of Belgium. In addition small row-crop tractors came into use, partly as a result of labor shortage, but also because of increased mechanization in general. Thus did draft-horse breeding come upon very hard times, and almost the end of the line. For a couple of years during the early 1950s the numbers fell to under two hundred horses.

Thankfully, though, those times have changed and the mid-eighties have proved to be the best years in the breed's history with the Belgian horse in the forefront and at prices fully recovered from those sad years of decline.

Cowboy poet and horseman Bo Bowman writes of the sorrow his grandfather experienced when he had to sell his great team of heavy horses. Here is his true account:

Heavy Horses

It's a phrase you sometimes hear, said in jest or on the fly
In a punch line, joke or story: "Ever seen a grown man cry?"
When that happens, I almost tell them how that memory
*   haunts my dreams!*
"Friend, I once saw a barnful, the day Grandpa sold his
*   teams."*

We might be at the feed store, or a café after a sale;
With a sympathetic listener, I might lean back and tell
*   the tale.*
I wasn't much more than a button, back in nineteen-fifty-nine,
When Grampa realized his dreams couldn't stop the march
*   of Time.*

Progress had reared her greasy head, roared her triumph's
*   loud exhaust;*
Plus he wasn't getting younger, and knew his cause was lost.
Tractors now swarmed the countryside, machinery made
*   the rules,*
Making hay with horses was left to a few hardheaded fools.

He couldn't stand to be there, to see them in the ring;
Bad health and prices forced him to do this dirty thing.

His partners of a lifetime, his workmates on the ranch,
Should retire to tall-grass pastures, but he didn't have that
    chance.

All the men there knew him, and knew his teams by name;
So when they entered through the gate, they felt his private
    shame.
They pranced in shoulder up to shoulder, their big heads held
    up proud,
As if harness had still joined them, and a hush fell on the
    crowd.

The auctioneer lost his voice, men got something in their eye;
Painful silence fell upon the crowd as those Percherons went by.
For there is nothing like the beauty of two life partners, side
    by side,
Sleek and proud and powerful, pulling at an easy glide.

I'd never seen 'em step like that when they were rakin' hay!
It seems they knew their future hung on how they looked
    that day.
They circled once more round the floor, each a mirror of the
    other,
Five well-matched and gentled teams: dam, sire, sisters,
    brothers.

The breast of each and every man was filled with such
    remorse,
For no creature God created has "heart" like a heavy horse.
As the feathered hooves dug in the dirt the gathered throng
    well knew
The heyday of the draft horse was just about all through.

In the silence of that moment, through the PA system's hum,
Each man pondered in his heart on what the horse has done.

Knights in heavy armor, who needed a stout steed,
The hardy serf's good helpmate, to plow and plant his seed.

Cities built, rivers dammed, bridges trussed up high,
Artillery and caissons, and war-bound troop supplies.
To carve and pile this modern world, the big horse was a
    factor;
Why, I'd bet it took horsepower *to build the world's first*
    tractor!

All this was quietly pondered by the men around that ring,
To the sound of heavy snortin' and the song those big shoes
    sing.
Every man knew in his heart, as those teams pranced through
    the gate;
Hard choices sure can scar a man, and bad ones seal his fate.

They were a breed of western men these days, you rarely meet;
I guess they figured they were next to be branded obsolete.
They grew up with heavy horses, worked them on their bottom
    land,
Could close their eyes and visualize the ribbons in their
    hands.

In that barn on that long-ago day, as the big hooves rose
    and fell,
Each man recalled past partnerships with teams they'd had
    to sell.
Those men had one thing I admired: they weren't too proud
    to cry;
I often think about them now, when I see a big horse go by.

You may think a tough old cowboy is not supposed to cry;
It's true they wouldn't bawl out loud, tears streaming from
    their eyes.

But stockmen are a mushy breed, bighearted to their roots,
And might sniffle, or blow real hard, or stare down at their
  boots.

Eventually, the magic stopped, the announcer found his voice;
The dog food buyer's made their bid, the hammer rang the
  choice.
Afterwards, his friends asked Gramps if it's true the deed was
  done;
As he just hung his silver head, they said "Damn. I'm sorry,
  Tom."

I'm told he gave the money to charity, as amends;
He couldn't stand to benefit from sellin' off his friends.
He died in his sleep the following year, hearing harness in his
  dreams;
I know he's up in Heaven now, makin' hay with his Percheron
  teams.

—BO BOWMAN
COLUMBUS, MONTANA

Interestingly, the reason for the increase in interest in the draft horse today is partly due to its mythology. "Smaller is better" does not apply here, but the beauty of the draft, which was once overlooked and was considered to be "behind the times," is now welcomed as an advertising vehicle and as a symbol of power and abundance. As "weekend farms" increase, so does the need for the great horse of old.

Nostalgia plays a role in this resurgence, as does the image of the Belgian—the big powerhouse horse that retains the drafty middle, the deep, strong foot. The great horse with a lot of bone and heavy muscle. The equine of amiable disposition that carries his knight enthroned on high. This, truly, is the Belgian. And of all the legends that surround him, here is one of the oldest and best.

During the ninth century A.D., there lived a knight named Renaud. He was walking in the forest one day when he met an old man who told him of a wild horse.

"This animal goes wherever it wishes, and it tramples our gardens and defiles our paths. Even the trees shiver when it comes near."

"I should like to see this horse," Renaud said. Already he wanted to tame the creature and have it for his own.

"There is but one way," the old man warned, mysteriously. "You will have to throw the horse to the ground."

Renaud's eyes gleamed. To capture a horse so magnificent would be a great prize for the young knight. And he believed he could do it.

While they stood and talked, the two men heard a huge noise in the forest, as if trees were being broken by a big wind. When Renaud peered through the dappled shade, he saw something. He looked again, and out of the darkness of the dense woods, a black horse burst into the view.

Renaud ran at it and the horse reared up, whinnying his challenge.

Then the two faced each other.

At first, the great horse pawed the air, then he delivered well-aimed blows with his hooves, but Renaud was quick, and he dodged them deftly.

In time, the horse grew tired and his wild blows fell upon the empty air because Renaud was never in the same place at the same time—he was everywhere at once.

And he had great stamina.

Finally, diving and rolling under the horse's ambush of hooves, Renaud caught the beast's right front leg and threw him flat to the ground.

Instantaneously, the horse changed. He got to his feet slowly and with much docility. Renaud looked deeply into his eyes and saw that the horse was his. The once-mad eyes were sad and calm, and Renaud saw the wisdom of the ages in them. So great was the horse's mind that he could hear his thoughts.

"You have conquered me, I am yours."

So Renaud named his mount Bayard and took him to Charlemagne's court, where he was the envy of all the other knights.

Bayard was like no horse that ever was, for he could understand human speech and was so strong he could carry four men at once.

With Bayard at his command, Renaud grew stronger than anyone except the king. Therefore, it was not long before the two men quarreled. Not long after that, Renaud was cast out of the king's castle. He and his three brothers fled to the forest of the Arden, where they built their own fort.

They fought against Charlemagne's army until they ran out of food and then, once more, they fled—only this time they went even deeper into the forest. Bayard remained great and strong, feeding on medicinal herbs and tubers and roots.

After a while, Renaud and his brothers were joined by another relation, a cousin named Maugis, who had magic powers. The five men rode to Poitier, where they entered the service of King John.

Now, at this same time, Charlemagne announced a horse race for which the prize was to be silver coins and his golden crown. Charlemagne was certain that no one could beat his favorite knight, Roland.

In order to disguise his appearance, Renaud asked Maugis to change him into a fifteen-year-old boy, which was done. In addition, Maugis cast another spell and made Bayard into a beautiful white charger. Now the two were completely changed, so that no one would know who they were.

When they got to the place where the contest was going to take place, Maugis took out an invisible silk thread. With it, he bound Bayard's leg so that he looked quite lame. The bad leg was so convincing that one of the knights of Charlemagne said, "A sad horse presented by a hopeless lad."

And the others nodded.

Now, before the race started, Maugis snipped the invisible silken binding, and Bayard, except for his whiteness, was himself again. At the blow of the horn, the knights spurred their mounts and the race began, but before the other horses could get up to stride, Bayard had crossed the ribbon and won.

Grinning from ear to ear, Renaud, still a mere lad, accepted the golden crown from the hand of his enemy, Charlemagne.

In doing so, he said, "Do not be so easily deceived—I am Renaud, and this is my horse Bayard."

Then he whirled around and galloped off into the woods. Charlemagne, openmouthed, saw his golden crown disappear into the leaves, but he was so surprised, he let out a small sigh. But no more than that was heard from him.

Thus began a war that lasted for many more years. Finally, however, Renaud and his men were reduced to starvation by the surrounding armies of the king. There was no food to eat in their fort, so they killed and devoured all of their horses except Bayard. In the end, if the men were to live, Bayard would also have to fall, but when the time came, Renaud, sword in hand, couldn't do the deed.

He dropped to his knees and wept. "I cannot kill you, dear friend," he said.

Then he made a small incision in the great horse's neck, and the drops of blood flowed from it. And Renaud and his brothers and Maugis lived off these droplets for four days, after which time, on the fourth night, they escaped the fort on the back of Bayard and eluded Charlemagne's army once again.

There came a time, however, when Charlemagne himself wanted the long war to be over, and he sent a scroll to Renaud by messenger that said that if he, Renaud, would surrender Bayard to him, the war would be done.

Renaud, after talking it over with his family, decided to give up his great horse at last. Tearfully, he did so, and the long war was declared over by Charlemagne. Yet the king's heart still burned with rancor, and no sooner did he have the great horse than he gave orders that a millstone should be tied to Bayard's neck and he should be thrown over the bridge of the River Meuse.

"At last I shall revenge myself on my ancient enemy," Charlemagne laughed as he witnessed the execution.

Over the bridge went Bayard with an enormous crash and a veil of spray. Below the surface, the invincible horse pounded the millstone with his hooves and ground it into grains of sand. Then he swam, underwater, away downriver where he would not be seen. And from then on, he lived, wild and free, as he had in the beginning.

Charlemagne never got satisfaction from either vanquishing Renaud or killing his horse Bayard. For now, on full-moon nights, there came a whinny on the wind—and there was Bayard, silhouetted, silver-edged, against the sky.

For centuries after this, farmers in the Ardennes Forest saw his tracks, and some declare that even today you can *hear* him neighing when the moon comes up over the rise.

No one has *seen* Bayard, except in dreams, for more than eleven hundred years.

A knight wearing light chain mail was a heavy load and hard going for the horse that toted him. Yet, add to this burden—plate armor on top of the chain mail—sword, lance, saddle, and weighty accoutrements, and the total had to be hellish indeed, even for a massive great horse.

Or if, unimaginably, it wasn't, consider that the easy way to have a man unhorsed was to kill or disable the horse itself. Thus did many equines go to the ground. To prevent this, another load was laid onto the horse's burden—more metal: chain mail drapery for the horse and trappings on top of that. So, in the end, the sturdy animal was as mobile as a mountain. No wonder the great horse had to be so indubitably great.

The noble knight was himself a stone-weighted thing whose gilt gear consisted of shoes of steel, steel greaves and knee-pieces secured with knots of gold, cuisses to protect the thighs, and a further encasement—a coat of fine mail complete with braces, elbow pieces, and gloves of plate. Finally, his coat armor richly made and put upon him, off he goes, golden-spurred, to do battle with a dragon or a bad neighbor.

After the battle, a man might find himself on a horse litter. This was a boxlike thing without wheels, a sort of buckboard used to drag off the dead and dying. It had a roof and was pulled by a horse.

A dying man lying in one of these probably prayed for a hair shirt and bed of nails. If a truly *great* great horse died in battle, he might also wind up on one of these litters, putting not the *cart* but the *horse* before *himself*, the horse—of course.

The Characteristics of the Belgian

The modern Belgian usually is more than sixteen hands and often exceeds eighteen hands. The average weight is between 1,800 and 2,000 pounds. Some stallions have weighed in at more than 2,400 pounds. A very docile, willing worker, he has a short neck and large head with muscular legs. The feet have minimum feathering, and the color is chestnut or roan with a blond mane and tail. The Belgians are the most numerous of all heavy breeds in the United States, and they have been chosen as the team to promote Coors beer products.

25

Pura Raza Española

ANDALUSIAN

native of the Iberian Peninsula and a product of the purest Spanish blood, the Andalusian is like her name—romantic.

The Iberian bloodline is made up of the Barb, the Arabian, and the Spanish horse—the foundation stock for all European equines. But it's the Andalusian, the favored mount of William the Conqueror and El Cid, that most people agree is the Spanish horse in quintessential form.

Originally, the Andalusian was a warhorse, the carrier of well-armed, heavily armored men. In addition to great strength and courage, this equine was, according to the duke of Newcastle in 1667, "the noblest horse in the world, the most beautiful that can be . . . great spirit and of great courage and docile; hath the proudest trot and the best action in his trot, the loftiest gallop . . . the lovingest and gentlest horse, and fittest of all for a king in his day of triumph."

Traces of the Andalusian go back to cave paintings, some of which were discovered on the Iberian Peninsula more than thirty thousand years ago. Homer mentions the Iberian mount in the *Iliad* (1100 B.C.), and William the Conqueror rode one into the Battle of Hastings (A.D. 1066) Still, the most famous Andalusian is Babieca, the horse of El Cid.

There are many folktales about how Babieca came to be the Cid's chosen favorite. In one tale, El Cid, who was the leader of the *Reconquista* (the rebellion that overthrew the Moors after seven hundred years of occupation), got the horse as a gift from his godfather, a priest known as Peyre Pringos, or Fat Pete.

The priest offered young Cid whatever horse he wished from the finely bred animals of the monastery. Supposedly, young Cid selected an awkward and dancy but otherwise unremarkable colt. Exasperated with the boy's choice, the friar shouted, "Babieca!," which means *stupid*—yet no one knows whether he was referring to his godson or the horse.

The second version of the legend states that El Cid won his equine in a fair fight. The king of Seville, who was on his way to meet El Cid, was mounted on a beautiful white horse trapped with purple and gold. Silver bells jingled from his reins; jewels sparkled from his bridle band. The king had come to take back Valencia by force.

Seeing his opponent, El Cid said, "The Moor seems to have come to a tournament instead of a battle. I will thus run a tilt with him that he will not soon forget. Whosoever wins this shall get Valencia *and* the proud white horse that carries the king so grandly."

The next day the battle in the garden of Villa Nueva routed the Moors and pushed them all the way to the river of Xucar, where, it is said, "they drank plenty of water without liking it." In the end, some fifteen thousand were drowned.

Now, the king of Seville escaped with his life, yet, as El Cid had said, he left behind his Iberian warhorse. So El Cid retained Valencia, won an historic victory, and became the new owner of a great charger. Some say Babieca refers to the vanquished king, but others say the name was given otherwise. For instance, James Baldwin *(The Horse Fair)* writes that "it was not derision that his master called him Booby, but by way of endearment."

In any event, for thirty years Babieca carried El Cid to one conquest after another, until the man and his horse became the stuff of legend. In his final fight with the Moors (A.D. 1099), again at Valencia, El Cid lost his life. However, his men dressed him for battle, as he himself had decreed. So, on the back of his old horse, which danced and held his head high, the great hero met his enemies for the last time.

Dead, El Cid rode out in gleaming armor, shield and sword knotted in hand, exactly at midnight. Behind the warrior came twelve hundred knights, all cloaked in white.

Fooled by the figure of the leader whom they had earlier seen mortally wounded, the Moors ran off while shouting, "El Cid is risen!" Balladry tells how he plowed through the tide of spreading men all the way to the monastery of San Pedro de Cardena. There he was taken off his horse and finally put to rest in the earth he loved.

As for Babieca, the horse lived on, unridden, for two and a half years after his master's death. Babieca died in A.D. 1101, having attained the remarkable age of forty.

■　　■　　■

The spirit of the Andalusian was once commonly used in rituals to ward off "the evil eye." That ceremony is still practiced today in some parts of the world. The way it is done, a stag's horn is attached to a cord made from the tail of a black mare. This is worn about the neck of a person who believes he is the victim of witchcraft. Now, fully protected, when an evil glance falls upon him, the wearer knows about it because the stag's horn breaks apart in the witch's presence.

Children wore Andalusian-staghorn charms into the 1950s in Seville. The little horns were silver-tipped and winked in the sunlight. Throughout the Middle Ages, horseback riders carried not stag-horns but pieces of turquoise, which kept their mounts from getting overtired and also protected the horsemen from falling.

Horses were once used to uncover other sources of evil in European society. There is still a widespread belief in vampires in some parts of Europe, particularly in the rural eastern region. According to a very old practice, a virgin youth (a male) was placed upon a black stallion, and he rode around a cemetery that was under suspicion of harboring vampires. If the horse stopped in front of a certain grave, it was exhumed and the corpse was pierced with stakes and then burned.

In certain parts of Yugoslavia, when this custom was banished by the government, the community resorted to civil disobedience to protest the ruling. Thus, the old rite was never outlawed with any kind of success. Another echo of this rite recently appeared in a modern Romanian vampire film. Obvously the rite has not been expunged from the mythos of central Europe.

26

The Literature of the Horse of Europe

he tale "The Tangle-Coated Horse" is from that matchless cycle of legendary Irish kings called *Tuatha De Danann*. Irish poets, dramatists, and storytellers have borrowed and remade these themes for centuries, John Millington Synge and *Riders to the Sea* being just one example. Perhaps the most entertaining stories in the saga are those of Finn MacCool. This next story, filled with Gaelic humor and irony, is a good example of the runic attempt to bring the worlds of Overland and Underwave, Earth and Under-Sea, together as one. The medium for this exchange—the unifier of all earthly and unearthly planes, including life and death, reality and dream—is the horse. The tangle-coated horse, as the story explains, is very closely aligned with the mystic unicorn. And the unicorn, mythologically speaking, is the sister of today's horse. No wonder our belief in magic horses has gone unchanged for so many centuries; there is no animal alive better suited to fit the bill, to carry us off to fabled lands of the imagination.

The Tangle-Coated Horse

Fionn, son of Uail, sat on a hillside that had the greenness of spring. All about the hillside were Fionn's men, hunters and warriors, each and every one. And as they built their fires and roasted their meats and talked among themselves, Fionn, their chieftain, sprawled in the grass and listened.

And this, in part, is what he heard.

"Well," bragged Cunnaun, "I am the man that knows the points of a horse."

"And what a choice it would be," said Diarmid, "a big-boned beast who would plant himself like a tree and not move until the biting-flies of summer noon grew as large as he."

"My horse would be big, no lie," vowed Cunnaun, "for slender is as slender does, and we have no need for wasted little things hereabouts, now, do we?"

Diarmid, to gain the upper hand, so to say, sang out in a high, lilting voice, at the end of which he neighed like a horse. Whereupon something in the forest answered him.

All sat up and were still, then—Cunnaun and Diarmid and the others at their tasks, and, of course, their leader, Fionn. All sat and listened. The high screaming as of a kelpie, or perhaps even a banshee, answered back across the realms of oak and the bowers of leafy green.

"Upon my word!" exclaimed Diarmid, as into the clearing there lumbered a big, shambling, rambling, rumbling tangle-coated horse. The earth fairly shook with each large flat-footed step, and the horse walked up and presented himself with something of a grin on his uncomely face.

"Don't hurry yourself, my jewel," said Diarmid.

"Try kindness on my horse, if you will," put in Cunnaun, and he approached the hairy beast slowly and with open hand.

The giant horse moved not a muscle.

Diarmid said, dry as barley, "What a knock-kneed monster with a bellows for breath and the bones of boulders and the brains of a straw of grass."

"Take the edge off your tongue," advised Cunnaun.

"I would give a roasted boar salted and stuffed with garlic, a haunch of venison, and a vat of mead to see you mount that shaggy beast," said Diarmid.

"In due time," answered Cunnaun, stroking the tangle-coated's broad nose. Then he added, "There be great power in honeyed words," and, speaking softly in the animal's huge ear, he suddenly vaulted lightly upon his back and took up a great grip of his mane.

The horse stood still as a stone.

"Do not hurry yourself, my treasure," said Cunnaun cheerfully. He glanced about proudly at the faces of the men, who watched him warily and openmouthed, all standing and ready with their spears should the great beast explode or do something otherwise unaccountable, which they thought it might.

But nothing of the kind happened.

"It may be," Cunnaun said after a time, "that he needs to feel the bulk of a rider who has more stones than I. Humor me, men, let's all sixteen of us climb up here now and see if he feels a bit more like moving then."

The others cried out in derision. None wanted any part of the horse's ill-jointed backbone.

"You cannot bribe them with half the world," called out Fionn, laughing.

Yet Cunnaun, who had an answer for everything and everyone, replied sharply, "Have you not heard tell of the kelpie that, having not gotten the better of a man, yields up his golden treasure?"

Now, all the bran-haired louts knew that tale and knew it well.

They looked at one another and nodded all round in agreement. And there was not one who was unafraid of the unknown, especially when a glint of gold was mentioned in the offing. So, reluctantly at first, but unhesitating at second, each of the sixteen warriors found a place on the back of the brute, and sidled up as they were, and holding on to the man in front, they all, in unison, gave the giant horse a kick in the ribs.

What happened is legend, history, mystery, magic, and a lesson all rolled into one. For that splayfooted piece of misfortune, that weighty-limbed, deep-chested, shaggy-coated horse rattled those riders like dry sticks in a high wind. He shook them like barley on the winnowing floor. He went across valleys and through trees and over rivers and into caves and out of ravines and around and over and between mountains until there was no Emerald Isle left to traverse, and then that tangled-coated horse came to the sword-bright sea and plunged into the surf and disappeared. All the while, Fionn, for whom there was no room on the horse's back, had clung to his tail; and as he held on for dear life, he cried out, "The sea will stop him," but as the sea did not, and as they— all sixteen—were under the sea, they held their breath.

Down, down they went, plodding along the seafloor, and at last they came to a great, ghostly bubble, sparking like crystal, and this the tangle-coated horse plunged right through to the other side, which was a world set apart.

Here, in the world of the bubble, which did not break but merely admitted them and closed behind them, was a land of ancient trees under which the shadows lengthened, and there was fine grass, and a singing lake, and murmuring bees, and the beauty of the place bore heavily on the mounted men, and they dismounted so as to see it better and with a clearer eye.

Twilight it was in that world, and everything stained and burnished with a dusky butterfly-winged goldish hue. There were mysterious spaces between every tree and cavernous depths that begged to be explored and lights that twinkled and expired. The men staggered about as if newly born, or, as was the case, reborn with a babe's glowy eyes in their wearisome heads.

After a spell, while the men moved around, glad and mad and all but spent, they began to see what lived there and what was natural to the place.

And what they saw amazed them.

For out of the branny bush came milk-white unicorns and moon-white stags. Gilded trees with leaves of silver gleamed and hung fully draped and sagging with fruits of crimson and ruby and apple-red. All round a soft radiance leaked between the higher, hoary trees that formed a rooftop overhead, above which, twinkling, was a sky of frosted fire, glittering and dazzling their eyes.

Suddenly, the amazed men heard a voice.

"A thousand welcomings to Fionn and his men!"

And there crowded forth a fabulous lot of handsome folk, men, women, and children, like jewels or stars—people they were, but fantastic people with light coming out of them.

"Tell us what you are and we will tell what we are," said Fionn, standing back a bit and stroking his chin while keeping his other hand firmly atop the hilt of his sword.

The brightest candle of the lot came forward. He was a man, tall and bearded like other men, but the light that came off and out of him was the most silver of all, and it shone and lapped just like flame. "I am called Silver Flame," he said, "and we are the people of Underwave."

Now, Fionn and his men had heard tales of such folk, and their land they had heard of, too—a place of lost, ancient, envied, starlit beauty that all mortals dreamed of seeing.

"Fate or good fortune has brought us thither," Fionn announced to Silver Flame, and he offered him his hand, which the other took. An instant radiance sparked out of Silver Flame's palm, and it filled the clearing with boundless good light, and all who were there, the Underwavelings and the Earthlings, felt it equally and were wonderfully enriched by its lapping and overlapping goodness.

Then did Fionn's warlike hand come away from his sword hilt, and he blinked as if stunned in the bath of effulgence that covered all in silvery star-flocks.

"Pulse of my heart," said Silver Flame, "you are welcome here, as we have besought you many a time and sent you messages of all kinds through the wee folk that inhabit both our worlds. Long have we dreamed of laying eyes on you, and long have you not come to the Land of Underwave."

Fionn, still clasping the gleam of Silver Flame's palm and filled with *light now himself, exhaled mightily. He felt the spirit of love enter his chest. As long as he kept hold of Silver Flame's hand, he heard the music of harps.*

"And how," asked Silver Flame, whose bright beard sparked when he spoke, "did you come hither, my lovely mortal-eyed man?"

"Came . . . I . . . thus?" Fionn's speech was staggered as he felt a new range of bubbly tickles course through his blooded veins. His knees buckled under the spell and his heart leaped apace.

Then he answered, "We came upon this woebegone, shaggy-coated horse." For a moment, he took his right hand away from Silver Flame's left and gestured at the huge horse. But the monstrous beast was not there. In its place, standing stock-still, was the grandest horse any man had seen. Gone was the tangled coat; gone the mule-tall ears; gone the bony bones, all loose and misplaced.

"What do I see in his place?" mumbled Fionn, and he looked to Cunnaun and Diarmid to gain their assent, their equal disbelief. Yet, they shrugged and shook their pates and wrinkled their brows. It was all too new to them, and their dumbstruck heads could barely take it in.

"What you see here is Earthshaker," said Silver Flame, and the dimness was chased away when he put his arm on Fionn's hard shoulder.

The horse that stood before them was every bit as large as the other that had brought them here, but this animal was clean of limb and aglimmer with flesh of silver. In all ways, he was comely, and his eyes shot forth with kindness and love and a magnitude of feelings, all good and right and godly, toward all men on earth.

"Is it . . . just a trick, then?" asked Fionn, trembling. "Am I dreaming?"

"Have you no other word for it than that?" asked Silver Flame.

"I can scarcely put a soft tongue to such hard-edged human thoughts, for you see, we believe that when goodness is so great, so large as to overwhelm a man, then it must, it just has to be a trick . . . or a dream."

"Cannot an Earthling just dream on and on, as we do here, not coming out of the dream, not ever?" queried Silver Flame, amused.

"Nay," said Fionn. "As long as you pin me to the spot, we are yours, but as soon as you release me from your spell, I shall be me again, full

of doubt and wonder and longing and unanswerable feelings of a human kind."

"I see," said Silver Flame, "that it is so. And that is why I have given you my horse Earthshaker, for whenever you doubt your dream, all that you need to do is climb upon his beautiful back and he will dream you off to here."

The great silvery stallion neighed in answer to this, shaking his mane so that a snowy light as at moonset on a winter's night twittered and glittered everywhere all round.

"So it is farewell now for a little," Silver Flame said. "You cannot stay but a while, otherwise your doubts will increase. But you shall not lose or forget Underwave. And we shall be close to you always. And when you win a victory up above, know that we are strengthening your hand. Think of us then on the slope when the antlered stag escapes you and when your enemy draws nigh and when, any time, you feel deserted and alone and lacking in love, which is just another word here for magic."

And so it happened that Fionn, knowing the truth of Silver Flame's wisdom, beckoned his men to get astride the great, white, glimmery stallion, Earthshaker, who was bridled with gold and wore golden bells on his bridle rein and who forthwith brought them back in a twinkling to the up-above world where, it is said, he changed, that horse did, to his old, shambly, oafsome self. And they say that only when the need for belief came up would he change into his other form, his heart-shaped perfection of love, just love. Yet they also say that those who believe the worlds are one—Overwave and Underwave—that they alone see the dream-filled wonder of the misshapen and the misbegotten, all things too big or too small, too hot or too cold, too bright or too dark, they alone see the tangle-coated horse as he really is—Earthshaker, the perfect bubble that does not break.

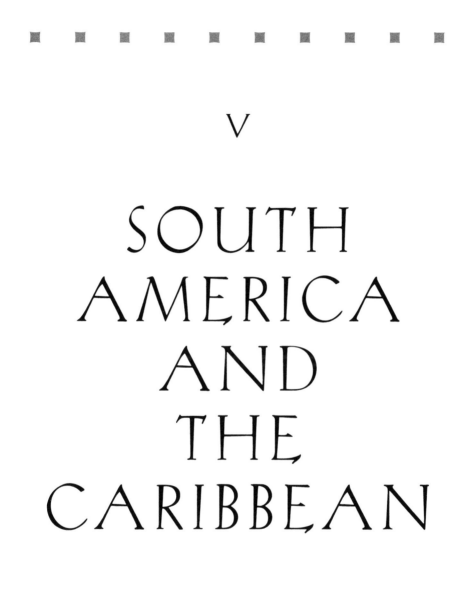

V

SOUTH AMERICA AND THE CARIBBEAN

27

The Fine–Step Horse

PASO FINO

The paso fino is the by-product of Christopher Columbus's discovery—not of the New World, but the land's lack of horses when he got there. He couldn't imagine such a thing, but there it was. So, on returning to Santo Domingo two years later, he brought plenty of equines with him, and he seeded the Western Hemisphere with a select group of mares and stallions that in time became the breed known as paso fino.

The horses Columbus brought on his second voyage were a mixture of bloods—Barb, Andalusian, and Spanish jennet. Their genes over the centuries melted down into a strong, capable, beautiful, four-beat gaited horse. They say that the paso fino's endurance and power come from the Barb, his grace from the Andalusian, and his gait from the jennet.

It is the latter that got the horse an international name and an impeccable reputation. This horse's fine step can be a walk or a collected canter, but it is always smooth—a broken pace that is lateral, not diagonal. The four beats are well pronounced, with equal intervals between each hoofbeat. As there is little vertical movement in the croup or the shoulder of the horse, the rhythmic flow is liquid and light.

Although the paso fino is known today to be useful, a workhorse as well as a play and show animal, it was originally a fighting equine called upon for conquest and exploration. Selectively bred for more than five hundred years, this breed became equally adaptable to rodeo, dressage, and endurance riding. Yet many say that the horse's unique value is as a family pet.

Audrey Pavia, writing in *Horse Illustrated*, tells about her great-great-grandfather's Peruvian paso stallion. The paso springs from the same Spanish stock as the American-bred paso fino, but is a separate breed. Still, the petlike qualities are obvious in this story.

> The air was dry and sweet as the chestnut stallion gaited freely along the trail. He had no rider, and didn't need one. He knew exactly where he was going.
>
> Before long, the four-beat rhythm of his rapidly moving

hooves clickety-clacked in the cobblestoned courtyard of the hacienda. As he approached the house, with its adobe walls and Iberian archways, he slowed to a walk.

The large glass doors to the dining room were open, just as he knew they would be, left ajar to allow the soft summer breeze to fill the house. The stallion pushed the doors open all the way with a flick of his muzzle, and confidently stepped inside. Nearly tiptoeing on the shiny terra-cotta tile floor, he made his way to the huge mahogany table that stood in the center of the dining room. Once his chest touched the table's edge, he stopped, seeing that which he had come for. Craning his neck out, he dipped his velvet muzzle into the sugar bowl, and began chewing contentedly, his job well done.

The literary myth of "the horse in the house" is an enduring one. It has been the subject of children's books, fantasies, and legends throughout the world. Horse-owner Jacqueline Tresl, in *Pets: Part of the Family*, writes of her fourteen-hundred-pound, spaghetti-eating equine, who, once allowed in the house, never left it. Single-digit temperatures started the trend, the author says, but "twelve years later, she's still here."

Tresl goes on to say,

> Housebreaking her was easy. Every four hours, day and night, I led her outside, urging her to "poop" and "pee." As soon as she did, I brought her back indoors and rewarded her with a cookie, apple, or (her favorite) a cream-filled donut. My husband built and attached a horse-sized porch onto our kitchen, then invented a double-swinging door that Misha could push open to go in and out. By the time she was eighteen months old, she had mastered the concept of letting herself out through her door when she had to do her business.

Some horses live half in the house by sharing the comfort zone of human food or doing things that seem a little unaccountable from a normal standpoint. In reality, horses enjoy being *with* us rather than being of service *to* us. Lifetime horse owner Dianne Tidwell relates some of her early experiences with this phenomenon.

As a farm child born just after World War II, my memories of horses go back to age two. Fascination for these magnificent animals began long before I had any comprehension of their power, their beauty and grace. Two Welsh ponies were my constant companions from age six. One loved to get at the dog's dish, but cherry pie was her favorite food and she would smear it all over her bald striped face whenever she got the chance. The other pony would do almost anything for a stolen sugar cube—this included ringing a doorbell and opening a gate (which got me into much trouble when she let other animals out of stalls).

As I grew older, my appreciation for horses grew into an obsession. Windcrest Magic, our pleasure gelding, loved soda pop, without ice—as an aged gelding, he was missing a few caps on his back teeth and cold things like ice cubes really hurt.

WM wasn't shy about checking out whatever he could steal from an unsuspecting owner or observer. He was known to dexterously lift Dumbo's Ears, hot dogs (minus the mustard), Oreo cookies, and all other normal horse treats, like carrots and apples. He did this with the consummate skill of a trained pickpocket.

When WM showed well at a horse show, he expected his usual soda vendor to be in the stall barn waiting for him. But he would get in line at the stand and wait his turn for a half glass of soda in a paper cup. Happily, WM would walk back to his stall with bubbles on his face and a paper cup held tightly between his front teeth. WM would also throw a temper tantrum if the trip to the soda stand was missed for any reason.

On a recent trip to Indianapolis, we met a horse owner whose Thoroughbred had a mouth so "soft" she could unscrew a lightbulb without breaking or damaging it. She would arch her neck, get her lips on the bulb when it was not turned on, delicately unscrew it, and then plop it into her water bucket. She would do this all day if given the opportunity.

Unless you are a horse owner, you cannot fully appreciate the dexterity this trick requires. It was something of an occupation with the Thoroughbred, too. But when we suggested the horse was trying "to say something," our acquaintance asked what that might be. We answered that the horse probably wanted a PC with very big keys and access to the Internet.

In the children's book *The Horse Who Lived Upstairs* by Phyllis McGinley, the discontented, vegetable-pulling wagon horse named Joey dreams of living in the country. As it is, he rides an elevator to his apartment on the fourth floor of a brick building in New York City.

There he has a window to look out of, oats to eat, straw to lie down in, and a bathtub to drink out of. But these things do not please him because Joey has his heart set on country living.

Given the chance to be a happy farm horse, however, Joey longs for life back in the city. He yearns for his cranky elevator, his stall, his tub. This story, published in 1944, has a horseshoe's ring of truth to it. It makes us wonder, as do all such tales, if horses would enjoy living as we do or whether they are just adaptable to our life, or the life being lived, whatever and wherever it is.

Actually, one of the gouty Hapsburg princes of Prague was so bloated and lame that he decided to house his horse on the second floor of his palace. When we visited his former mansion, now a music school during the day and a restaurant at night, we ascended the same stone stairs that led to the prince's great bedroom and horse stall. The stairs did not seem as wide as we'd imagined, not large enough for the huge equine that we'd also imagined going up them.

When we asked about this, Jan Wiener, a history professor from Charles University, explained, "Shirley Temple Black, in her office as the U.S. ambassador to Prague, remade each stair to its pre-Hapsburgian dimension—a terrible shame, we think—but so very American."

But despite the alteration, going up the stairs that first night, we had the feeling of what it must have been like riding a horse to a bedroom in the stars, and the sound of the hooves clattering on the grand echoing walls and halls. We wondered if, after a night of heavy drinking, the prince dropped off to sleep, on horseback, halfway between stair and heaven, neither up nor down, neither two-legged nor four-, astride a very ancient dream. The "horse in the house" is a mythical and literary tradition that probably began some two thousand years ago in a barn in Bethlehem. At any rate, it is the equivalent of dreaming on a ship in calm waters or sleeping under the stars on a cool summer's night.

There is something timeless, careless, and cuddly—if you are a child or a poet—about just being in a barn. Something thick and mysterious in the odor of dry, well-stored hay. A bit of poetry in knowing that horses of the night are in the darkness, in the magic of the breathing barn.

Recently, we spent the night at the New Marlboro Hunt Club in Massachusetts. Our well-appointed quarters were over the stable, and the horses were under us, whinnying and nickering all night long in the wintry air of the open barn.

We were warm under a down comforter, and the sounds the horses made were lulling and rapturous. The intermittent knock of a hoof or the dull bump of a heavy body brought back a haystack of memories.

It was much like falling asleep in a horse meadow where the cows came up to us in the dark thinking our white faces were salt licks. If you have never been licked by a cow or kissed by a horse with your eyes closed in the warm, syrupy thickness of half-sleep, you do not know what it is like to sleep in horsey heaven.

The Characteristics of the Paso Fino

A distinctive sense of refinement halos this horse of Columbus whose straight profile is lovely to see. The eyes are large and well spaced, and they give the horse the look of alert intelligence. The ears are short and close set. The gracefully arched neck is medium in length and set at an angle, which allows for a high carriage. The chest is moderate in width. The legs are straight, and the tail is carried high and very gracefully. The mane, tail, and forelock are excessively full and luxurious. The paso fino is small, not exceeding just over fourteen hands, and she grows slowly. The breed doesn't achieve full size until five years of age. Every color is found in this breed, with or without white markings.

The birthright of every paso fino is a four-beat gait, and some foals even try to take their first steps in gait. There are more than 200,000 paso fino horses registered in Central and South America. A confederation composed of Europe, the United States, Puerto Rico, Columbia, Venezuela, the Dominican Republic, Panama, and Aruba was formed for the purpose of competition. The Paso Fino Confederation has held three world cups since 1993.

A breed of wild horses on Abaco Island in the Bahamas has the same DNA as Spanish Barbs and paso finos. The origin of the horses was unclear until the late nineties, when historians decided that most of the herd came from Cuba, and thus from Spain. Prior to this, the theory was that the ancestors of the Abaco wild horse came from England.

28

The Literature of the Horse of South America and the Caribbean

According to author Robert D. San Souci, "The story of the seven-colored horse is popular throughout the Spanish-speaking world." He speaks of four versions in Puerto Rico, as well as French, Russian, and Israeli tellings. The scenery of the tale depends on many landscapes, from desert to mountain to rain forest—South America is definitely one of the major locations, if not the only one. Interestingly, the universality of the tale stretches, as Robert points out, as far east as Russia, and the version that is told there is called "Little Magic Horse." The same grim (and we should say, Grimm) brothers preside, but their father in the Russian version is also a trickster. The lovely girl is the sad-eyed daughter of the Moon, and the hero on his quest must elicit the aid of not only his (instead of the seven-colored equine, this one is a little humpbacked horse) pony, but also the fish of the deep and even a great whale. As one might imagine, the Russian story is quite complex and has elements of suffering missing in the warmer geographical renditions. If there was ever doubt that mortals regard horses as their betters, their masters in the physical and psychic realm, this tale sets the record straight.

The Little Seven–Colored Horse

BY ROBERT D. SAN SOUCI

Once upon a time a farmer arose early in the morning to work in his cornfield. To his dismay, the granjero *found that some beast had come by night and eaten many ears of corn. The husks of the* mazorcas *were scattered among trampled stalks.*

"Ay! Ay! Ay!" the granjero *cried. "We will be ruined!" His cries awoke his three sons. They gazed fearfully at the damage, wondering what sort of animal had ravaged their* maíz.

The man told his eldest son, "Diego, guard our cornfield tonight."

But Diego fell asleep during his watch. The next morning, the maízal *had been plundered just as before.*

So the angry granjero *told his second son, "Pedro, keep watch, and see that you do not fall asleep."*

But this lazybones soon nodded off; once again, their maíz *was eaten.*

Finally the youngest brother, Juanito, or little Juan, said, "Let me keep watch. I will not let anything get our maíz."

His brothers laughed at him, saying, "How can you do what we could not?"

But Juanito took a length of soga *and his guitar with him. He gathered the fattest* mazorcas *and piled them beneath a tree. Then he hid himself in its branches. With his rope close at hand, he strummed his guitar and sang softly to keep awake.*

At midnight, a caballito *galloped down from the sky into the cornfield. Juanito counted seven colors in the little horse's coat, but they never seemed to his eyes the same seven colors. They changed and changed again. The magical pony began to eat the* maíz *piled under the tree. Then Juan lassoed and captured it.*

To the boy's amazement, the seven-colored horse said, "I beg you to let me go. If you do this, I promise that I will always help you if you find yourself in trouble. Just call: 'Caballito de Siete Colores, *once, I set you free; now, Little Seven-Colored Horse, I ask you to help me.' And I will come to your aid."*

"First," said Juanito, "you must promise not to eat my father's maíz."

"I give you my word," said the horse.

So Juanito loosened the rope, and the horse galloped into the sky and vanished.

When Juanito told his father and brothers what had happened, they laughed and said, "You fell asleep and dreamed."

But the next night and every night thereafter the maíz *was left untouched. So the others realized that Juanito had told the truth.*

Then his brothers called him Bobo—"Foolish"—because he had not kept the wondrous seven-colored horse and sold it for a thousand silver reales. *Riches were always on the minds of these two. They hated the hard work tilling the soil, growing* maíz, *and carrying it to market. They dreamed of becoming wealthy so they would never have to work another day. Finally Diego said, "Father, I am going away to the city to seek my fortune."*

And Pedro said, "I am going with him."

"Let me go with you," begged Juanito, "and we will seek our fortunes together. When we are rich, we can buy a casa grande, *and have Father come live with us." But his brothers refused, and they went off without him.*

Still Juanito followed after them, sure they would not turn him away when they saw that he, too, was determined to find fame and fortune. He caught up with them on a bridge across a river.

"Hola!" he greeted his brothers.

"Hola!" responded Diego, giving Pedro a wink. Then Diego said, "Look, Juanito! There is something in the water!"

"Si," Pedro agreed, peering into the river. "Is it gold?"

But when Juanito bent down to look, his brothers pushed him into the swift-flowing stream.

"Adios, pescadito!" Diego called.

"Goodbye, little fish!" echoed Pedro.

Laughing and clapping each other on the back, they hurried off, giving not a single thought to poor Juanito, who was swept along by the river. Barely staying afloat, Juanito clutched at every rock until he managed to grab hold of a tooth of rock in midstream. Too tired to swim to shore, he almost gave up hope. Then he remembered what the magical horse had told him. So he called out:

Caballito de Siete Colores,

Once, I set you free;

Now, Little Seven-Colored Horse,

I ask you to help me.

Instantly the horse galloped down out of the sky. He raced atop the river as though the rushing water were solid as the king's highway. When he reached Juanito, the boy climbed onto the pony's bare back, clinging to his mane.

"Where shall I take you?" asked the horse.

"To the city," said Juanito, "to seek my fortune."

"Very well," said the seven-colored horse. As they flew south and east, Juanito suddenly caught a floating dark blue pluma, tipped with silver.

"Toss that feather away," said the horse, "or it will bring you bad luck."

But Juanito said, "Surely something this pretty can only bring me good luck." And he stuck the jaunty pluma in his cap. Soon Juanito saw the city beneath them. The horse flew down to the ground. When the boy had dismounted, the pony returned to the clouds. Juanito went to an inn, where he asked the innkeeper, "Might there be a job for me here?" The innkeeper hired Juanito to sweep the patio and fetch water and wash dishes. In return, he gave Juanito a bed and some frijoles and arroz.

As he ate his beans and rice, Juanito heard two serving girls talking about María, the beautiful daughter of the city's alcalde, Don José Éscobar. The girl had so many suitors, they said, that she was unable to choose among them. So she had decided to wed the man who won the sortijas, the tournament of rings. The contest was to be held on Sunday *after mass; all unmarried men of the town, including the hidalgos, each the son of a wealthy don, would compete for María's hand.*

On Sunday, Juanito asked to go and watch the tournament. But the innkeeper said, "First you must finish all your chores." Though there was work enough for two, Juanito swept and scrubbed and polished so that he finished in next to no time. Then he called:

Caballito de Siete Colores,

Once, I set you free;

Now, Little Seven-Colored Horse,

I ask you to help me.

This time the horse came with a saddle and reins of the finest leather, inlaid with gold and silver. Tied in a bundle to the silver pommel was a dark-blue velvet jacket, trousers with silver buttons and embroidery, suede boots decorated with peacock-blue silk thread, and a magnificent sombrero.

Juanito climbed upon the back of the little seven-colored horse.

Off they trotted to the plaza, where a crowd had gathered to watch the young men try to win the hand of María, the mayor's daughter.

The instant Juanito saw her all dressed in white, walking beside her father, she captured his heart. When she was seated under an awning, the alcalde signaled for the contest to begin.

Astride the seven-colored horse, Juanito looked more dashing than any other rider. María spotted him at once, and asked her father, "Who is the hidalgo on the fanciful horse?"

But her father did not know.

Now, Juanito's brothers, Diego and Pedro, were also competing for María's hand. Recognizing his brother, Diego said, "Juanito Bobo, what are you doing here on an underfed mount that does not even know what color a proper horse should be?"

Juanito sat up proudly in his saddle and said, "Hold your laughter until the contest is over."

"We will, Bobo," sneered Pedro. "Then we will laugh even louder."

The tournament began as the first riders took off. Holding their pommels with one hand, they used lances to try to catch rings of colored ribbon that hung above the length of the racecourse. Many riders—including

Juanito's brothers—came near to winning. But in the last race, to the crowd's cheers, Juanito snared all the rings.

Juanito rode to Maria, dismounted, removed his sombrero, and knelt before her, holding out his lance with its rainbow of rings. "Dona María, I present this to you; and I present to your father my claim for your hand in marriage." María smiled warmly and fluttered her fan prettily. But before the alcalde could reply, Pedro and Diego pushed through the crowd. They were furious that Juanito had won the contest.

"Don José," said Diego, bowing low, "do you see the elegant pluma in our brother's hat? Only this morning, Juanito vowed that if he won the race, he would fetch the bird from which it came and give it to your daughter as a gift."

"Is this true?" asked the alcalde.

Before Juanito could deny it, Pedro said, "Si, I heard him say this very thing."

Then María said, "Would you do this for me?"

Helpless before her dark eyes and bright smile, Juanito could only say, "Whatever you wish."

Soon after this, Juanito set out toward the south, riding the little seven-colored horse. Some distance from the city, the horse said, "See, Juanito? I told you that pluma would bring bad luck. Now we face a long, dangerous search to find that bird."

"I am sorry, amigo," the boy said, stroking the horse's mane. "I should have listened. I won't have you risk yourself because of my foolishness. Go! I will seek the bird on my own."

"Nonsense," said the horse. "Friends don't desert friends. You have learned your lesson, so let's be off."

They flew over deserts of hot white sand, snowcapped blue mountains, and forests a thousand shades of green that stretched as far as Juanito could see. At last they came to a laguna, whose waters and tree-lined shores were thronged with birds of every size and color: parrots, macaws, toucans, flamingos, and countless others. As they flew down toward the lagoon, the birds rose up in waves of color, screeching and slashing at them with beaks and talons as sharp as daggers.

"The bird you seek is king of these creatures. Use this sword to defend yourself," said the horse. Juanito found a golden sword fastened to the pommel of his saddle. With it, he defended them from the angry birds. After a fierce battle, the winged army flew off. Then the horse carried Juanito to the southernmost shore of the laguna. *The moment his hooves touched the ground, the sword in Juanito's hand became a golden cage. Nearby, Juanito saw a marvelous bird, its deep blue feathers tipped with silver. It was so ancient it could no longer fly. Juanito felt such pity, he could not touch it.*

But the bird said, "I am old and weary, and long to cross the skies one last time. Take me with you, and let me see the world from above once more."

Gently, Juanito set the bird in the cage. Then the horse and rider began their long journey home.

Now, while Juanito was away, Diego and Pedro (who were to be María's brothers-in-law) were granted important positions in the household of the alcalde. There they learned that years before, the King of Spain had sent a priceless gold ring, studded with diamonds, emeralds, and rubies, to Don José in thanks for his royal service to the crown. But the ship that carried the ring had been sunk by a storm before reaching shore.

The moment that Juanito presented the wondrous bird to his beloved María, Diego and Pedro took the alcalde aside.

"Don José," said Diego, "our brother has promised us that he will fetch you the golden ring that was lost at sea."

Then Pedro added, "He hopes that you will let him bestow it on your lovely daughter as a memoria."

The delighted alcalde announced that Juanito had promised to recover the lost ring as an engagement present for María. Snared by his brothers' lies, Juanito agreed to the seemingly impossible task. Alone, Juanito walked to the shore and gazed hopelessly over the waves. Though he felt even the little horse could not help him this time, he called:

Caballito de Siete Colores,

Once, I set you free;
Now, Little Seven-Colored Horse,
I ask you to help me.

Soon the loyal steed raced down from the sky. When Juanito had explained the challenge set for him, the horse said, "Hold fast to the pommel and don't let go for an instant, or you will drown." Then the horse raced into the sea. As the waves closed over his head, Juanito clung to the silver pommel with both hands. To his surprise, he found that he could breathe the water as easily as air. The seven-colored horse carried him through waving green forests of algas marinas and living curtains of bright-colored peces that parted before him. Far ahead, in the blue-black water, Juanito saw a golden gleam, no bigger than the head of a pin.

"That is the ring," the horse told him, "but you will need even more skill than you showed at the tournament of rings to snatch it from the creature that guards it."

Juanito could see that the gleaming spot lay in the shadows of a sunken ship. On either side, the wooden ribs curved like the walls of a church. At first, it seemed that the golden ring rested on a small hill. Then, to his horror, Juanito saw that the hill was actually a giant langosta. The golden ring was caught on one antenna of the monstrous lobster.

As soon as horse and rider were close enough, the langosta began snapping its saw-toothed pinzas at them. The deadly claws went snick-snap, snick-snap. The horse circled the creature, darting close then backing off, leaping over just out of reach of the huge pinchers.

"Use one hand to seize the ring," said the horse. "But hold the pommel with the other, or you will drown."

Again and again, Juanito tried to capture the prize. But the fearsome sea-beast moved so quickly and used its pinzas so skillfully, that—snick-snap—it nipped Juanito's arms and legs many times. Growing weary, Juanito said to the little horse, "Draw out the monster one last time. I have a final plan." Obediently, the horse charged at the creature, then retreated. Snick-snap, went the pinzas of the langosta as it rushed forward. Snick-snap. Snick-snap.

Suddenly, Juanito let go of the pommel. The monster, all of its attention on the little seven-colored horse, did not move quickly enough as Juanito arced above it, tugged free the golden ring, and swam for the surface. But the moment Juanito let go of the pommel, his lungs filled with water. Still he swam up and up, clutching the ring, even as he felt himself drowning. Then the little seven-colored horse was beside him. Juanito grabbed the pommel with his free hand. Instantly, he could breathe.

The two galloped across the waves, beyond the shore of the house of the alcalde. There, Juanito presented the gold memoria *to his beloved María. Diego and Pedro glared at their brother as they made their way toward the alcalde with more mischief in mind. But Juanito quickly said, "Don José, my brothers told me that they wish to carry your greetings to the King of Spain, and share the happy news of the ring's recovery."*

"Bueno!" *cried the alcalde, embracing Diego and Pedro. "You set sail for Spain tomorrow morning."*

The brothers spent half the voyage blaming each other for what had happened. After that, they decided that they were destined to find their fame and fortune at the Spanish court. What befell them history does not record. It is enough to know that they never returned to trouble Juanito and María, who were married and lived quite happily. They invited Juanito's father to come and live with them, and he became the closest friend of the alcalde. The couple built the little seven-colored horse a splendid stable, and he remained their loyal companion for the rest of their days.

Bibliography

Absjornson, Peter Christian & Moe, Jorgen. *Norwegian Folk Tales.* New York: Pantheon, 1960.

Anderson, J. K. *Ancient Greek Horsemanship.* Berkeley and Los Angeles: University of California Press, 1961.

Berman, Lucy. *Famous Horses.* New York: Golden Press, 1972.

Boone, J. Allen. *Kinship with all Life.* New York: Harper & Row, 1954.

Botkin, B. A. *A Treasury of Southern Folklore.* New York: Crown Publishers, 1949.

Catlin, George. *Letters and Notes on American Indians, 1832–1839.* London: N.p., 1841.

Chih-Yi & Plato Chan. *The Good-Luck Horse.* Eau Claire, Wis.: McGraw-Hill, 1943.

Cirlot, J. E. *A Dictionary of Symbols.* New York: Philosophical Library, 1962.

Conn, George H. *The Arabian Horse in Fact, Fantasy and Fiction.* New York: A. S. Barnes, 1963.

Dargon, Olive Tilford. *The Welsh Pony.* Boston: Privately printed for Charles A. Stone, 1913.

Dobie, J. Frank. *The Mustangs.* New Jersey: Castle Books, 1952.

Dorrance, Bill & Desmond, Leslie. *True Horsemanship Through Feel.* Novato, Calif.: Diamond Lu Productions, 1999.

Dumas, Phillipe. *The Lipizzaners and the Spanish Riding School of Vienna.* Saddle River N.J.: Prentice-Hall, 1981.

Edwards, Elwyn Hartley. *The Encyclopedia of the Horse.* New York: D.K. Publishing, 1994.

———. *Horses: Eyewitness Handbooks.* New York: D.K. Publishing, 1993.

Eisenberg, John. *The Longest Shot: Lil E. Tee and the Kentucky Derby.* Lexington: University Press of Kentucky, 1996.

Emery, Joan & Vavra, Robert. *On Horses.* New York: William Morrow, 1984.

Fonseca, Isabel. *Bury Me Standing: The Gypsies and Their Journey.* London: Vintage, 1996.

Ferber, Edna. *Giant.* New York: Doubleday, 1952.

Fletcher, Sidney. *The Big Book of Cowboys.* New York: Grosset & Dunlap, 1973.

Geddes, Candida. *The Complete Book of the Horse.* London: Octopus Books, 1978.

Graham, Cunningham. *The Horses of Conquest.* Norman: University of Oklahoma Press, 1949.

Graves, Robert. *The White Goddess.* New York: Farrar, Straus & Cudahy, 1948.

Hanners, Laverne. *Girl on a Pony.* Norman: University of Oklahoma Press, 1994.

Hausman, Gerald. *The Kebra Nagast: The Lost Bible of Rastafarian Wisdom and Faith from Ethiopia and Jamaica.* New York: St. Martin's Press, 1998.

————. *Meditations with Animals: A Native American Bestiary.* Sante Fe: Bear, 1986.

Hendricks, Bonnie. *The International Encyclopedia of Horse Breeds.* Norman: University of Oklahoma, 1995.

Henry, Marguerite. *Album of Horses.* Chicago: Rand McNally, 1961.

————. *Brighty of the Grand Canyon.* Chicago: Rand McNally, 1980.

————. *King of the Wind: The Story of the Godolphin Arabian.* Chicago: Rand McNally, 1964.

Hogner, Dorothy Childs. *The Horse Family.* New York: Oxford University Press, 1953.

Holling, Holling Clancy. *The Book of Cowboys.* New York: Platt & Munk, 1936.

Hopkins, Andrea. *Dolorous Gard: Chronicles of King Arthur.* New York: Penguin Books, 1993.

Howey, M. Oldfield. *The Horse in Magic and Myth.* New York: Castle Books, 1968.

Humphries, Rolphe (translator). *The Gypsy Ballads of García Lorca.* Bloomington: Indiana University Press, 1963.

Jacobson, Patricia & Hayes, Marcia. *A Horse Around the House.* New York: Random House, 1999.

Janus, Sharon. *The Magic of Horses: Horses as Healers.* Hygiene, Colo.: Sunshine Press, 1997.

Jennings, Philip S. *Medieval Legends.* New York: St. Martin's Press, 1983.

Kenrick, Vivienne. *Horses in Japan.* London: J. A. Allen, 1964.

Khury, Samantha. *Samantha Khury: I Talk to Animals.* Videocassette. Produced and directed by Peter Friedman. New York: WLIW, 1991.

Larousse Encyclopedia of Mythology. New York: Prometheus Press, 1959.

Law, Robin. *The Horse in West African History.* London: International African Institute, 1980.

Lawrence, Elizabeth A. *His Very Silence Speaks: Comanche—the Horse That Survived Custer's Last Stand.* Detroit: Wayne State University Press, 1989.

Maeterlinck, Maurice. *The Unknown Guest.* Secaucus, N. J.: University Books, 1975.

McCormick, Marlena & von Rüst, Adele. *Horse Sense and the Human Heart.* Deerfield Beach, Fla.: Health Communications, 1997.

McDowell, Bart. *Gypsies: Wanderers of the World.* Washington, D.C.: National Geographic Society, 1970.

McGinley, Phyllis. *The Horse Who Lived Upstairs.* Philadelphia: J. B. Lippincott, 1944.

McGuane, Thomas. *Some Horses.* New York: Lyons Press, 1999.

Meltzer, Milton. *Hold Your Horses.* New York: HarperCollins, 1995.

Morris, Desmond. *Horsewatching.* New York: Crown Publishers, 1988.

Mellin, Jeanne. *The Morgan Horse Handbook.* Brattleboro, Vt.: Stephen Greene Press, 1973.

Pace, Mildred. *Old Bones, the Wonder Horse.* New York: McGraw-Hill, 1956.

Peterson, Cris. *Horsepower: The Wonder of Draft Horses.* Honesdale, Pa.: Boyds Mill Press, 1977.

Pittenger, Peggy Jett. *Morgan Horses.* New York: Arco Press, 1972.

Pony Boy, Gawani. *Horse Follow Closely: Native American Horsemanship.* Irvine, Calif.: Bowtie Press, 1998.

Rashid, Mark. *A Good Horse Is Never a Bad Color.* Boulder, Colo.: Johnson Books, 1996.

Raswan, Carl. *Drinkers of the Wind.* New York: Ariel Books, 1964.

Reader's Digest Association. *Marvels and Mysteries of Our Animal World.* Pleasantville, N.Y.: Reader's Digest Press, 1964.

Roberts, David & Krakauer, Jon. *Iceland: Land of the Sagas.* New York: Harry Abrams, 1990.

Roberts, Monty. *The Man Who Listens to Horses.* New York: Random House, 1997.

———. *Shy Boy: The Horse That Came in from the Wild.* New York: HarperCollins, 1999.

Rodanas, Kristina. *Dance of the Sacred Circle.* Boston: Little, Brown, 1994.

Rosen, Michael J. *Horse People: Writers and Artists on the Horses They Love.* New York: Workman Publishing, 1998.

San Souci, Robert D. *The Little Seven-Colored Horse.* San Francisco: Chronicle Books, 1995.

Saroyan, William. *My Name Is Aram*. New York: Harcourt Brace, 1937.

Serruys, Henry. *Kumiss Ceremonies and Horse Races*. Wiesbaden, Germany: Otto Harrassowitz, 1974.

Seton, Ernest Thompson. *Wild Animals I Have Known*. New York: Grosset & Dunlap, 1967.

Shub, Elizabeth. *About Wise Men and Simpletons: Twelve Tales from Grimm*. New York: Macmillan, 1971.

Smith, Elinor Goulding. *Horses, History and Havoc: Through the Ages with Hoof in Mouth*. New York: World Publishing, 1969.

Steiner, Stan. *Dark and Dashing Horseman*. San Francisco: Harper & Row, 1981.

Stewart, Michael. *The Time of the Gypsies*. Boulder, Colo.: Westview, 1997.

Summers, Patti. *Talking to Animals*. Charlottesville, Va.: Hampton Roads, 1998.

Tietjens, Eunice. *The Romance of Antar*. New York: Coward McCann, 1929.

Tellington-Jones, Linda. *Getting in TTouch: Understand and Influence Your Horse's Personality*. North Pomfret, Vt.: Trafalgar Square Publishing, 1995.

Van der Linde, Laurel. *From Mustang to Movie Stars: Five True Horse Legends of Our Time*. Brookfield, Conn.: Millbrook Press, 1995.

Vernon, Arthur. *The History and Romance of the Horse*. New York: Dover Publications, 1939.

Wear, Terri A. *The Horse's Name Was . . . A Dictionary of Famous Horses from History, Literature, Mythology, Television and Movies*. London: Scarecrow Press, 1993.

Winning at the Track: How to Pick 'Em. Reseda, Calif.: Increase Video, 1994.

Witter, Rebekah Ferran. *Living with Horsepower!* Pomfret, Vt.: Trafalgar Square Publishing, 1998.

Wylder, Joseph. *Psychic Pets: The Secret World of Animals*. New York: Stonehill Press, 1978.

Yagan, Murat. *I Came from Behind Kaf Mountain*. Putney, Vt.: Threshold Books, 1984.

Yuasa, Nobuyuki (translator). *Basho: The Narrow Road to the Deep North and Other Travel Sketches*. London: Penguin, 1968.

Zelazny, Roger. *Sign of the Unicorn*. New York: Avon Books, 1975.

Permissions Acknowledgments

Grateful acknowledgment is made to the following for permission to reprint previously published and unpublished material.

BRUCE N. BOWMAN: Poem "Heavy Horses" by Bruce N. "Bo" Bowman. Reprinted by permission of the author.

SID HAUSMAN: Portions of "Joe Rivera Interview," stories "A Horse to Make Justin Proud," "Ten Appaloosas," "Wagons, Horses and Helicopters," and discussions of "Sven." Reprinted by permission of the author.

INDIANA UNIVERSITY PRESS: "The Comical History of Don Pedro, Knight" from *The Gypsy Ballads of Garcia Lorca*, translated by Rolfe Humphries. Reprinted by permission of Indiana University Press.

THE LYONS PRESS: Excerpt from *Some Horses* by Thomas McGuane. Copyright © 2000 by Thomas McGuane. Reprinted by permission of The Lyons Press, an imprint of the Globe Pequot Press, Guilford, Conn., 1-800-962-0973, www. globe-pequot.com.

DAVID MCKAY COMPANY: Excerpts from *The Tangle Coated Horse and Other Stories* by Elizabeth Young. Copyright 1929 by Longmans, Green & Co. and renewed in 1957 by Elizabeth Young. Reprinted by permission of David McKay Company, a division of Random House, Inc.

AUDREY PAVIA: Excerpt from "Peruvian Hoofbeats" from *Horse Illustrated* by Audrey Pavia. Reprinted by permission of the author.

KAREN RICKENBACH: "Sir William's Irish Taffy" by Karen Rickenbach. Reprinted by permission of the author.

ROBERT D. SAN SOUCI: *The Little Seven-Colored Horse* by Robert San Souci. Reprinted by permission of the author.

DIANNE DAVIS TIDWELL: Untitled Windcrest Magic Story by Dianne Davis Tidwell. Reprinted by permission of the author.

WARDEN MUSIC CO., INC.: Song lyric "Tennessee Stud" by Jimmy Driftwood. Copyright © 1958 by Warden Music Co., Inc. Renewed 1986. All rights reserved. Reprinted by permission of Warden Music Co., Inc.

Index

About the Authors

GERALD and LORETTA HAUSMAN have been writing about animals for many years. They came naturally to this book, for each of their families was horse owners, with various specialties in the field. Loretta's father was a member of the last Cavalry Corps in the United States Army. Gerald's mother was an equestrian who got Gerald and his brother, Sid, on horseback soon after they could walk. Sid became a professional horseman, Gerald a writer of animal stories. Previous books by Gerald and Loretta Hausman are *The Mythology of Dogs* and *The Mythology of Cats*, which have been translated into a variety of foreign languages and have been widely reviewed. Gerald spends much of the year telling animal stories to children in schools and at camps and book festivals.